POETICA 20

Apollinaire: Selected Poems

T0159757

Also by Oliver Bernard

SELECTED POEMS

Apollinaire

Translated and introduced by

Oliver Bernard

ANVIL PRESS POETRY

New edition published in 2004
by Anvil Press Poetry Ltd
Neptune House 70 Royal Hill London SE10 8RF
www.anvilpresspoetry.com
Reprinted in 2013

First published in 1965 by Penguin Books Ltd
Expanded, bilingual edition published in 1986
by Anvil Press Poetry Ltd

ISBN 978 0 85646 359 4

This book is published
with financial assistance from
Arts Council England

A catalogue record for this book
is available from the British Library

Designed and set in Monotype Dante by Anvil
Printed and bound in Great Britain
by Hobbs the Printers Ltd

In memory of Robert Colquhoun
and Robert MacBryde

M. Apollinaire seems to have decided to become the trustee of all the faults of all the superannuated schools of literature. To complete his singularity he has removed ... all the punctuation from his work. Throughout these 200 pages one looks in vain for a comma ...

Georges Duhamel (15 June 1913) on *Alcools*

M. Guillaume Apollinaire stands out among the young writers as an engaging eccentric. I prefer to think of him as a very subtle scholar who likes to amuse himself and who is not afraid to show his taste for the bizarre ... 200 pages without a stop or comma. But at least we are repaid for our effort: Guillaume Apollinaire is a charming poet ... There are very few slipshod pages ... in fact, several really moving lines ...

Henri Martineau (July 1913) on *Alcools*

Thank you, thank you for your article, thank you for appreciating my poems. However, it is not the bizarre which pleases me, but life, and when one knows how to look around one sees the most curious and interesting things. As regards the punctuation, I cut it out simply because it seemed to me unnecessary; which in fact it is, for the rhythm itself and the division of the lines are the real punctuation, and nothing else is needed ...

Apollinaire to Martineau (1913)

As for the calligrams, they are an idealization of vers-libre poetry and of typographical precision at a time when typography is brilliantly ending its career, at the dawn of new methods of reproduction, the cinema and the gramophone ...

Apollinaire to André Billy (1918)

I do not know whether a critic may one day depict him as gay or sad, serious or frivolous, virtuous or a libertine, a believer or an atheist, a bourgeois or a revolutionary: for he was all these things at once ...

Marcel Adéma: *Apollinaire le Mal-Aimé* (1952)

Apollinaire occupies an eminent position in modern poetry: an increasing number of works are devoted to him, the University concerns itself with him, and he is in a fair way to becoming a classic.

Marcel Adéma & Michel Décaudin: Foreword to
Apollinaire: Œuvres Poétiques (Gallimard, 1956)

Here, then – and let us at least admit it – is Apollinaire, labelled Baroque Poet, standing before us as the man best qualified to represent the Baroque in modern times. Are we farther advanced by this? . . . However full of meaning it is, a single word can hardly exhaust the possibilities of describing a reality as rich and complex as that which nourishes a great poet's inspiration – and, Baroque or not, Symbolist or not, Apollinaire is first and foremost a great poet . . .

André Billy: Preface to the above work (1956)

THE PRESIDENT AND MEMBERS
OF THE MUNICIPAL COUNCIL OF PARIS
HAVE THE HONOUR TO REQUEST
YOUR ATTENDANCE ON
FRIDAY 9 NOVEMBER, 1951, AT II A.M.
AT THE INAUGURATION OF THE RUE
GUILLAUME-APOLLINAIRE

MEETING-PLACE: AT THE
CORNER OF RUE SAINT-BENOIT   ADMIT
AND RUE DE L'ABBAYE   ONE

Contents

Introduction

GUILLAUME-ALBERT-WLADIMIR-ALEXANDRE-APOLLINAIRE Kostrowitzky – the poet Guillaume Apollinaire – was born in Rome on 26th August 1880, the illegitimate son of Mlle Olga de Kostrowitzky, a Polish adventuress of noble birth, and Francesco Flugi d'Aspermont, an officer in the Bourbon army.

His education was received in Monaco and Nice: from the age of ten onwards he was, to all intents and purposes, French. Between the ages of ten and fifteen he won twenty prizes for scholarship (including drawing) – most of them firsts. He did not, however, win French nationality until he had served both in the artillery and the infantry: from December 1914 (when he enlisted as a private in the artillery) to March 1916 (by which time he had re-enlisted as a sub-lieutenant of infantry). Eight days after the decree according him French nationality appeared in the *Journal Officiel*, a shell splinter pierced his steel helmet and entered his skull in the region of the right temple. Trepanned, he survived to be promoted lieutenant (temporary acting) in June 1918; but he was not yet fully recovered when he succumbed to influenza in the Paris epidemic of November. His funeral took place in a city still reeling from victory celebrations. Some of his friends said they kept thinking all those flags must be for him.

'My dear André,' wrote Cocteau to the poet André Salmon at midnight on the 9th–10th November, 'Poor Apollinaire is dead – Picasso is too sad to write . . .' Thirty years later a member of the Académie Goncourt, in his introductory essay to an Apollinaire selection[1] which is still in print, was to say: 'Where he is concerned I feel very strongly that criticism is not my *forte.*'

The man whose person and whose performances inspired these expressions is not yet well known in England; and among those who know anything of him at all there are probably as many painters as poets. For very good reasons: Apollinaire was the first writer to understand what the cubists were up to. He championed Braque, Matisse, Vlaminck, and Derain long before the art critics realized

---

[1] *Poètes d'aujourd'hui*, No. 8, *Apollinaire*, selected and introduced by André Billy. Pierre Seghers, 1947.

their worth. His first book of poems, the *Bestiaire*, is embellished with some of the best work Dufy ever did. A portrait of him painted by his friend the Douanier Rousseau shows him standing beside yet another painter, his second great love, Marie Laurencin – to whom he was introduced in 1908 at Picasso's instigation. Already in 1905, in order to make Picasso known to the public, Apollinaire had written in support of his work some of the most 'prophetic and lyrical' art criticism in modern times.

For obvious reasons French painting travels faster – and more safely – than French poetry. Nevertheless French poets do arrive in England, eventually. Rimbaud and Verlaine lived off the Tottenham Court Road in the 1870s, and returned as it were posthumously between the wars. Laforgue was smuggled in by Eliot. Baudelaire is always with us. Three later arrivals – Aragon, Prévert and Cocteau – point to the fact that Apollinaire has been skipped, somehow. But all of them have other claims to fame than their poetry. Aragon, whose work appeared here during the Nazi occupation of Europe, was a French Resistance man and a member of the French communist party. Jacques Prévert wrote not only poems but film scripts – among them such remarkable ones as that of Carné's *Le Jour se lève*. Cocteau, whose versatility is a byword, even received an honorary Doctor's Degree from the University of Oxford. Different as they all are, these last three poets would probably have acknowledged Apollinaire as a master – even as a more modern poet, sometimes, than themselves.

Apollinaire did, in fact, visit England more than once during his lifetime: one of the first things one learns about him is that his longest and one of his most marvellous poems[2] was written about his love for an English girl whom he met in Germany in 1901, and who eventually fled to America to escape his importunities. But he was only 38 when he died, and it was nearly another of his lifetimes before his biography appeared in English.[3]

The contrast between the relative obscurity of Apollinaire's reputation in Britain and the affection and admiration shown for his work in France is very marked. It is a fact that, there, 'the University

2 'La Chanson du Mal-Aimé (1909), see page 36.

3 *Apollinaire* by Marcel Adéma, translated by Denise Folliot. Heinemann, 1954.

concerns itself with him', and that original editions of his poems fetch impressive prices; but it is also true that he is 'the last of the poets whose lines young people know by heart' – 'one of the most French of our poets, in the pure tradition of Villon, of La Fontaine, of Gérard de Nerval, of Baudelaire, of Verlaine: a tradition which he himself enlarged to the farthest possible limits.[4]

I have already suggested one possible reason for this contrast, by mentioning the 'other claims to fame' of Cocteau, Prévert and Aragon. It is worth mentioning also the sensation one has when in Paris that Apollinaire is still alive: the tombstone and menhir in the Père Lachaise Cemetery notwithstanding. The memorial by Picasso in the garden next to the church of St Germain, opposite the Rue Guillaume Apollinaire, and almost opposite the *Deux Magots*, and – farther back along the Boulevard St Germain itself – the building where Apollinaire lived (on the corner of the Rue St Guillaume), really seem to be less reminders of the dead than of the living.

Living, too, seems the picture of Apollinaire that one obtains from the Adéma biography, and from the wealth of other material available. Not least the portraits: the primitive Rousseau painting with the idyllic setting; the severe Picasso drawing after a photograph taken in hospital; and all the photographs, notably a local photographer's full-length of Apollinaire in uniform, in which, he said: 'I have assumed the attitude of Mars when he has an appointment with Venus.' Living: at once confusing and precise. It is easy to *recognize* Apollinaire: a large man with a large head and slow movements; a rather grave face; a habit of putting his hand in front of his mouth when he laughs; a lover of contrasts, of the strange and the bizarre, and yet a person capable of extraordinary simplicity; a hearty eater and drinker; a lover; a scholar, or at least a curious seeker after knowledge; a person delighting in the company of others; a charming companion, and yet greedy of affection and very vulnerable to slights and indifference. Every fresh piece of evidence fits remarkably, considering the profusion of colours and contrasts: the deep sad voice on the record of 'Le Pont Mirabeau',[5] and the anecdote of

---

4 Preface to *Poèmes Apollinaire* by André Billy. Livre de Poche, 1963.
5 Obtainable from the Musée de la Parole, Rue des Bernardins, Paris Ve.
6 In 'The Song of the Ill-Loved'.

Apollinaire poking fun, five minutes earlier, at the instrument on which the recording was made; the tenderness and candour of the 'Song for Laetare'[6] and the violence of the 'Reply of the Zapur-Og Cossacks' a few lines farther on; the friendship between Apollinaire and his dug-out companions on the one hand, and his passion for the aristocratic 'Lou' on the other. André Billy discovered about Apollinaire the poet that the word best suited to describe him was 'Baroque'. It can equally be applied to Apollinaire the man. But 'Baroque' is only a label. If, thanks to M. Billy and others, it is easy to recognize Apollinaire, it is impossible to describe him: it is as if he will not keep still. M. Billy even declares that the Apollinaire 'legend' is false:

> For us who were his friends this legend does not exist: it never did exist. Let us not hesitate to say rather that Apollinaire was superior to it. He exercised at every moment during his short stay among us more gifts than have been spoken of. ... In order to speak properly of him one would need his own power of transfiguration. He transfigured himself when alive, and he transfigured in his own style everything that came within his reach. This power, together with his look, his smile, and his irresistible way of pleasing and of obtaining forgiveness, has not passed into the 'legend' but is gone forever.

*　　*　　*

THE POEMS in this book are translations from the text of the Pléiade edition *Apollinaire: Œuvres Poétiques* (© Éditions Gallimard 1959). Most of their originals are also to be found in the cheaper Seghers and Livre de Poche selections. Several, including 'Le dromadaire', 'La chêvre du Thibet', 'Rosemonde' and 'Bleuet', were – famously – set to music by Francis Poulenc; and there is or was a recording of Yves Montand singing 'Saltimbanques' to music by Louis Bessières.

Acknowledgements are due to Andrée Grandperret, Suzanne Gautherin, and Lucien Marchand, for much help and good advice. Also to Stephen Spender, during whose time as poetry editor of *Encounter* 'The Song of the Ill-Loved' and several other Apollinaire versions first appeared in its pages.

The present edition has been revised and slightly expanded. It now possesses the advantage of a facing French text. 'Les Fiançailles'

('The Betrothal') has been completed, and there are one or two poems which did not appear in the Penguin edition of 1965.

Since that time Apollinaire may be said to have arrived in Britain, and I should like to acknowledge in particular the very good edition of *Alcools* in the Athlone French Poets series (The Athlone Press, 1975) from which I have learnt a good deal.

OLIVER BERNARD

Orphée

Admirez le pouvoir insigne
Et la noblesse de la ligne:
Elle est la voix que la lumière fit entendre
Et dont parle Hermès Trismégiste en son Pimandre.

Orpheus

Marvel at this frank mastery
And these outlines' nobility:
This is the voice which the first light made heard
And for which Trismegistus found the word.

Zone

A la fin tu es las de ce monde ancien

Bergère ô tour Eiffel le troupeau des ponts bêle ce matin

Tu en as assez de vivre dans l'antiquité grecque et romaine

Ici même les automobiles ont l'air d'être anciennes
La religion seule est restée toute neuve la religion
Est restée simple comme les hangars de Port-Aviation

Seul en Europe tu n'es pas antique ô Christianisme
L'Européen le plus moderne c'est vous Pape Pie X
Et toi que les fenêtres observent la honte te retient
D'entrer dans une église et de t'y confesser ce matin
Tu lis les prospectus les catalogues les affiches qui chantent
        tout haut
Voilà la poésie ce matin et pour la prose il y a les journaux
Il y a les livraisons à 25 centimes pleines d'aventures policières
Portraits des grands hommes et mille titres divers

J'ai vu ce matin une jolie rue dont j'ai oublié le nom
Neuve et propre du soleil elle était le clairon
Les directeurs les ouvriers et les belles sténo-dactylographes
Du lundi matin au samedi soir quatre fois par jour y passent
Le matin par trois fois la sirène y gémit
Une cloche rageuse y aboie vers midi
Les inscriptions des enseignes et des murailles
Les plaques les avis à la façon des perroquets criaillent
J'aime la grâce de cette rue industrielle
Située à Paris entre la rue Aumont-Thiéville et l'avenue des Ternes

Zone

In the end you are tired of that world of antiquity

O Eiffel Tower shepherdess the bridges this morning are a
    bleating flock

You have had enough of living in Greek and Roman antiquity

Here even the motorcars look like antiques
Only religion is still quite new religion
Remains as simple as the airfield hangars

You alone in Europe O Christianity are not ancient
And the most modem European is you Pope Pius X
But shame restrains you whom the windows watch
From going into a church and confessing this morning
You read handbills catalogues posters singing aloud
That's what poetry is this morning and for prose there are the
    papers
There are 25-centime instalments full of detective stories
Portraits of the famous and a thousand assorted titles

This morning I saw a pretty street whose name I forget
It was the bright new herald of the sun
Directors and labourers and beautiful shorthand-typists
Pass through it four times a day between Monday morning and
    Saturday evening
There each morning the siren wails in groups of three blasts
An irascible bell in full cry sounds towards noon
And the signwriting and the writing on the walls
And the nameplates and the notices shriek like parrots
I love the gracefulness of this factory street
Which is situated in Paris between the Rue Aumont-Thiéville
    and the Avenue des Ternes

Voilà la jeune rue et tu n'es encore qu'un petit enfant
Ta mère ne t'habille que de bleu et de blanc
Tu es très pieux et avec le plus ancien de tes camarades René
    Dalize
Vous n'aimez rien tant que les pompes de l'Église
Il est neuf heures le gaz est baissé tout bleu vous sortez du
    dortoir en cachette
Vous priez toute la nuit dans la chapelle du collège
Tandis qu'éternelle et adorable profondeur améthyste
Tourne à jamais la flamboyante gloire du Christ
C'est le beau lys que tous nous cultivons
C'est la torche aux cheveux roux que n'éteint pas le vent
C'est le fils pâle et vermeil de la douloureuse mère
C'est l'arbre toujours touffu de toutes les prières
C'est la double potence de l'honneur et de l'éternité
C'est l'étoile à six branches
C'est Dieu qui meurt le vendredi et ressuscite le dimanche
C'est le Christ qui monte au ciel mieux que les aviateurs
Il détient le record du monde pour la hauteur

Pupille Christ de l'œil
Vingtième pupille des siècles il sait y faire
Et changé en oiseau ce siècle comme Jésus monte dans l'air
Les diables dans les abîmes lèvent la tête pour le regarder
Ils disent qu'il imite Simon Mage en Judée
Ils crient s'il sait voler qu'on l'appelle voleur
Les anges voltigent autour du joli voltigeur
Icare Énoch Élie Apollonius de Thyane
Flottent autour du premier aéroplane
Ils s'écartent parfois pour laisser passer ceux que transporte
    la Sainte-Eucharistie
Ces prêtres qui montent éternellement élevant l'hostie
L'avion se pose enfin sans refermer les ailes
Le ciel s'emplit alors de millions d'hirondelles
A tire-d'aile viennent les corbeaux les faucons les hiboux
D'Afrique arrivent les ibis les flamants les marabouts
L'oiseau Roc célébré par les conteurs et les poètes

And look what a young street it is why you are only a small
    child yet
Your mother dresses you only in blue and white
You are very pious too and like your oldest playmate René Dalize
You love nothing so much as the ceremonies of the Church
At nine o'clock the gas is turned down so low it burns blue and
    you slip out of the dormitory
To pray all night in the school chapel
While the eternal adorable amethyst depths
The blazing glory of Christ revolves forever
It is the lovely lily we all nurture
The redhaired torch the wind cannot put out
The pale and rosecoloured son of the dolorous mother
The evergreen tree of all prayers
The intertwined stems of honour and eternity
The sixpointed star
It is God who dies on Friday and is resurrected on Sunday
Christ climbing heavenward faster than aviators
Holder of the world altitude record

Christ apple of the eye
Twentieth pupil of centuries he can do it
And changed into a bird in this century how Jesus soars
The demons in the abysses raise their heads to look at him
They say he imitates Simon Magus of Judaea
They cry out even if he can fly he's only a fly-by-night
But the angels flutter about this bonny flier
Icarus Enoch Elijah and Apollonius of Tyana
Hover about the first aeroplane
Dividing from time to time to make way for those who are
    exalted by the Holy Eucharist
Those priests eternally ascending raising the Host
And at last the aeroplane comes down without folding its wings
And then the sky fills with millions of swallows
Crows and falcons and owls come winging
Ibis and flamingoes and marabou storks out of Africa
The Roc celebrated in fable and by poets

Plane tenant dans les serres le crâne d'Adam la première tête
L'aigle fond de l'horizon en poussant un grand cri
Et d'Amérique vient le petit colibri
De Chine sont venus les pihis longs et souples
Qui n'ont qu'une seule aile et qui volent par couples
Puis voici la colombe esprit immaculé
Qu'escortent l'oiseau-lyre et le paon ocellé
Le phénix ce bûcher qui soi-même s'engendre
Un instant voile tout de son ardente cendre
Les sirènes laissant les périlleux détroits
Arrivent en chantant bellement toutes trois
Et tous aigle phénix et pihis de la Chine
Fraternisent avec la volante machine

Maintenant tu marches dans Paris tout seul parmi la foule
Des troupeaux d'autobus mugissants près de toi roulent
L'angoisse de l'amour te serre le gosier
Comme si tu ne devais jamais plus être aimé
Si tu vivais dans l'ancien temps tu entrerais dans un monastère
Vous avez honte quand vous vous surprenez à dire une prière
Tu te moques de toi et comme le feu de l'Enfer ton rire pétille
Les étincelles de ton rire dorent le fond de ta vie
C'est un tableau pendu dans un sombre musée
Et quelquefois tu vas le regarder de près

Aujourd'hui tu marches dans Paris les femmes sont ensanglantées
C'était et je voudrais ne pas m'en souvenir c'était au déclin de
    la beauté

Entourée de flammes ferventes Notre-Dame m'a regardé à
    Chartres
Le sang de votre Sacré-Cœur m'a inondé à Montmartre
Je suis malade d'ouïr les paroles bienheureuses
L'amour dont je souffre est une maladie honteuse
Et l'image qui te possède te fait survivre dans l'insomnie et dans
    l'angoisse
C'est toujours près de toi cette image qui passe

Glides clutching Adam's head in its talons the first head of all
From the far horizon the eagle swoops uttering a great cry
And the small hummingbird comes from as far as America
And the long and sinuous pi-his come from China
They that have only one wing and fly by couples
And then the Dove the Immaculate Spirit appears
Escorted by the lyre bird and the eyed peacock
And the phoenix the self-engendering pyre
Veils everything for an instant with its burning ashes
The sirens leave the perilous passages of the sea
And arrive singing all three of them most marvellously
And all of them eagle phoenix and Chinese pi-his
Fraternize with the flying machine

And now you are walking all alone in Paris among the crowds
And herds of roaring omnibuses are rolling past you
The anxiety of your love clutches at your throat
As if you were never going to be loved again
If you lived in the old days you would enter a monastery
You feel ashamed when you catch yourself saying a prayer
You laugh at yourself and your laughter crackles like hellfire
The sparks of your laughter light up the depths of your existence
Like a picture hung up in a gloomy museum
And sometimes you go up close to it and look at it

Today you are walking in Paris and the women are covered with
    blood
This was and I wish I could forget it it was at the time of the
    failing of beauty

Surrounded by a fervency of flames Our Lady looked at me in
    Chartres
And in Montmartre the blood of your Sacred Heart drowned me
I am sick of hearing the blessed words
And the love from which I suffer is a shameful disease
And the image of you persists through anguish and insomnia
And when I am near you this image always passes away

Maintenant tu es au bord de la Méditerranée
Sous les citronniers qui sont en fleur toute l'année
Avec tes amis tu te promènes en barque
L'un est Nissard il y a un Mentonasque et deux Turbiasques
Nous regardons avec effroi les poulpes des profondeurs
Et parmi les algues nagent les poissons images du Sauveur

Tu es dans le jardin d'une auberge aux environs de Prague
Tu te sens tout heureux une rose est sur la table
Et tu observes au lieu d'écrire ton conte en prose
La cétoine qui dort dans le cœur de la rose

Epouvanté tu te vois dessiné dans les agates de Saint-Vit
Tu étais triste à mourir le jour où tu t'y vis
Tu ressembles au Lazare affolé par le jour
Les aiguilles de l'horloge du quartier juif vont à rebours
Et tu recules aussi dans ta vie lentement
En montant au Hradchin et le soir en écoutant
Dans les tavernes chanter des chansons tchèques

Te voici à Marseille au milieu des pastèques

Te voici à Coblence à l'hôtel du Géant

Te voici à Rome assis sous un néflier du Japon

Te voici à Amsterdam avec une jeune fille que tu trouves belle
       et qui est laide
Elle doit se marier avec un étudiant de Leyde
On y loue des chambres en latin Cubicula locanda
Je m'en souviens j'y ai passé trois jours et autant à Gouda

Tu es à Paris chez le juge d'instruction
Comme un criminel on te met en état d'arrestation

Now you are by the shores of the Mediterranean
Under the lemon trees which flower from year's end to year's end
You go for a sail with your friends
And one of them is a Nicean and one is a Mentonian and there
    are two Turbiasques
We look down in horror at the squids of the deep
And through the seaweeds Christ's fishes are swimming

You are in a garden in the suburbs of Prague
You feel very happy and there is a rose on the table
And instead of writing your prose story you look at the metallic
Sheen of the beetle asleep in the heart of the rose

Terrified you see yourself depicted in the agates of Saint Vitus
You were as sad as death the day you saw yourself there
You are like Lazarus driven mad by daylight
The hands of the dock in the Jewish quarter are turning backwards
And you are passing slowly backward through the history of
    your life
Climbing the hill to the Hradchin and listening in the evening
To Czech songs being sung in the taverns

Here you are in Marseille among the watermelons

Here you are in Koblenz at the Sign of the Giant

And here you are in Rome under a Japanese medlar tree

Here you are in Amsterdam with a girl whom you think beautiful
    and who is ugly
She is supposed to be marrying a student from Leyden
Where they let rooms in Latin CUBICULA LOCANDA
I remember it I spent three days there and as many at Gouda

Now you are in Paris at the Examining Magistrate's
They have placed you under arrest like a criminal

Tu as fait de douloureux et de joyeux voyages
Avant de t'apercevoir du mensonge et de l'âge
Tu as souffert de l'amour à vingt et à trente ans
J'ai vécu comme un fou et j'ai perdu mon temps
Tu n'oses plus regarder tes mains et à tous moments je voudrais
        sangloter
Sur toi sur celle que j'aime sur tout ce qui t'a épouvanté

Tu regardes les yeux pleins de larmes ces pauvres émigrants
Ils croient en Dieu ils prient les femmes allaitent des enfants
Ils emplissent de leur odeur le hall de la gare Saint-Lazare
Ils ont foi dans leur étoile comme les rois-mages
Ils espèrent gagner de l'argent dans l'Argentine
Et revenir dans leur pays après avoir fait fortune
Une famille transporte un édredon rouge comme vous
        transportez votre cœur
Cet édredon et nos rêves sont aussi irréels
Quelques-uns de ces émigrants restent ici et se logent
Rue des Rosiers ou rue des Ecouffes dans des bouges
Je les ai vus souvent le soir ils prennent l'air dans la rue
Et se déplacent rarement comme les pièces aux échecs
Il y a surtout des Juifs leurs femmes portent perruque
Elles restent assises exsangues au fond des boutiques

Tu es debout devant le zinc d'un bar crapuleux
Tu prends un café à deux sous parmi les malheureux

Tu es la nuit dans un grand restaurant

Ces femmes ne sont pas méchantes elles ont des soucis cependant
Toutes même la plus laide a fait souffrir son amant

Elle est la fille d'un sergent de ville de Jersey

Ses mains que je n'avais pas vues sont dures et gercées

J'ai une pitié immense pour les coutures de son ventre

You made painful and joyful journeys
Before you discovered falsehood and old age
You suffered love at twenty years old and at thirty
I have lived like an idiot and wasted my time
You no longer dare look at your hands and every minute I feel
    like sobbing
Over you over the girl I love and over everything that has
    terrified you

You are looking at the eyes of those emigrants which are
    brimming with tears
They believe in God they pray the women suckle their children
They fill the waiting room at the Gare St Lazare with their odour
They trust in their stars as the three wise men did in their star
They hope to make money in the Argentine
And go back to their own country with a fortune
One family carries an eiderdown with it as you carry your heart
This eiderdown and our dreams are equally unreal
Some of the refugees stay here and take rooms
In the Rue des Rosiers or the Rue des Écouffes in hovels
I have often seen them taking the air in the street in the evening
They move as slowly as pieces in a game of chess
Above all there are the Jews whose women wear wigs
And sit bloodlessly in the backs of their shops

You are standing in front of the counter in a low drinking place
Drinking a penny coffee among the unfortunates

You are in a great restaurant at night

Those women are not evil but still they have their troubles
Each one of them has made her lover suffer even the ugliest

Who by the way is the daughter of a policeman in Jersey

Her hands which I hadn't noticed before are hard and calloused

I feel a great pity for the scars on her belly

J'humilie maintenant à une pauvre fille au rire horrible ma bouche

Tu es seul le matin va venir
Les laitiers font tinter leurs bidons dans les rues

La nuit s'éloigne ainsi qu'une belle Métive
C'est Ferdine la fausse ou Léa l'attentive

Et tu bois cet alcool brûlant comme ta vie
Ta vie que tu bois comme une eau-de-vie

Tu marches vers Auteuil tu veux aller chez toi à pied
Dormir parmi tes fétiches d'Océanie et de Guinée
Ils sont des Christ d'une autre forme et d'une autre croyance
Ce sont les Christ inférieurs des obscures espérances

Adieu Adieu

Soleil cou coupé

Now I make a humble face for a poor girl with a horrible laugh

You are alone and soon it will be morning
Milkmen are banging their churns in the streets

Night passes away like Métive the Beautiful
Like Ferdine the False like Leah the Forlorn

And you are drinking spirits that burn your mouth as your life
      burns it
Your life that you toss off as though it were a glass of spirits

You are walking towards Auteuil you wish to go home on foot
To sleep among your South Sea Island fetishes and West African
      idols
Which are Christs of dissimilar forms and of other beliefs
Minor Christs of obscurer longings

Farewell Farewell

Beheaded sun

Le Pont Mirabeau

Sous le pont Mirabeau coule la Seine
      Et nos amours
    Faut-il qu'il m'en souvienne
La joie venait toujours après la peine

      Vienne la nuit sonne l'heure
      Les jours s'en vont je demeure

Les mains dans les mains restons face à face
      Tandis que sous
    Le pont de nos bras passe
Des éternels regards l'onde si lasse

      Vienne la nuit sonne l'heure
      Les jours s'en vont je demeure

L'amour s'en va comme cette eau courante
      L'amour s'en va
    Comme la vie est lente
Et comme l'Espérance est violente

      Vienne la nuit sonne l'heure
      Les jours s'en vont je demeure

Passent les jours et passent les semaines
      Ni temps passé
    Ni les amours reviennent
Sous le pont Mirabeau coule la Seine

      Vienne la nuit sonne l'heure
      Les jours s'en vont je demeure

The Pont Mirabeau

Under the Pont Mirabeau the Seine
  Flows with our loves
 Must I recall again?
Joy always used to follow after pain

  Let the night come: strike the hour
  The days go past while I stand here

Hands holding hands let us stay face to face
  While under this
 Bridge our arms make slow race
Long looks in a tired wave at a wave's pace

  Let the night come: strike the hour
  The days go past while I stand here

Love runs away like running water flows
  Love flows away
 But oh how slow life goes
How violent hope is nobody knows

  Let the night come: strike the hour
  The days go past while I stand here

The days pass and the weeks pass but in vain
  Neither time past
 Nor love comes back again
Under the Pont Mirabeau flows the Seine

  Let the night come: strike the hour
  The days go past but I stay here

La tortue

Du Thrace magique, ô délire!
Mes doigts sûrs font sonner la lyre.
Les animaux passent aux sons
De ma tortue, de mes chansons.

Tortoise

My certain fingers, brain of fire!
Strike the magic Thracian lyre.
The animals pass in a throng
Hearing my tortoise and my song.

Le cheval

Mes durs rêves formels sauront te chevaucher,
Mon destin au char d'or sera ton beau cocher
Qui pour rênes tiendra tendus à frénésie,
Mes vers, les parangons de toute poésie.

Horse

My hard and formal dreams will learn to ride you,
My destiny in its golden car shall guide you,
Holding as taut as madness reins: the rhymes
Written by me, all poets' paradigms.

La Chanson du Mal-Aimé

A Paul Léautaud

Et je chantais cette romance
En 1903 sans savoir
Que mon amour à la semblance
Du beau Phénix s'il meurt un soir
Le matin voit sa renaissance

Un soir de demi-brume à Londres
Un voyou qui ressemblait à
Mon amour vint à ma rencontre
Et le regard qu'il me jeta
Me fit baisser les yeux de honte

Je suivis ce mauvais garçon
Qui sifflotait mains dans les poches
Nous semblions entre les maisons
Onde ouverte de la mer Rouge
Lui les Hébreux moi Pharaon

Que tombent ces vagues de briques
Si tu ne fus pas bien aimée
Je suis le souverain d'Égypte
Sa sœur-épouse son armée
Si tu n'es pas l'amour unique

Au tournant d'une rue brûlant
De tous les feux de ses façades
Plaies du brouillard sanguinolent
Où se lamentaient les façades
Une femme lui ressemblant

The Song of the Ill-Loved

To Paul Léautaud

I was singing this romance
In 1903 not knowing my
Love is like the Phoenix if
One fine evening he should die
Morning sees him born again

One night of London mist and flame
A corner boy who looked like my
Lover came up and asked my name
But what I saw in that one's eye
Made me lower mine in shame

I followed this young dog who hands
In pockets whistled as he went
That street became the Red Sea sands
Open for him the Jews and meant
To drown me Pharaoh all my bands

Let these piled bricks fall ton on ton
If I did not love you then
I am a King of Egypt's son
His sister-Queen and all their men
If you are not the only one

At a corner of the street
That burned with all its signs alight
Like sores that fogs and acids eat
In old housefronts that weep all night
Like him but for her faltering feet

C'était son regard d'inhumaine
La cicatrice à son cou nu
Sortit saoule d'une taverne
Au moment où je reconnus
La fausseté de l'amour même

Lorsqu'il fut de retour enfin
Dans sa patrie le sage Ulysse
Son vieux chien de lui se souvint
Près d'un tapis de haute lisse
Sa femme attendait qu'il revînt

L'époux royal de Sacontale
Las de vaincre se réjouit
Quand il la retrouva plus pâle
D'attente et d'amour yeux pâlis
Caressant sa gazelle mâle

J'ai pensé à ces rois heureux
Lorsque le faux amour et celle
Dont je suis encore amoureux
Heurtant leurs ombres infidèles
Me rendirent si malheureux

Regrets sur quoi l'enfer se fonde
Qu'un ciel d'oubli s'ouvre à mes vœux
Pour son baiser les rois du monde
Seraient morts les pauvres fameux
Pour elle eussent vendu leur ombre

J'ai hiverné dans mon passé
Revienne le soleil de Pâques
Pour chauffer un cœur plus glacé
Que les quarante de Sébaste
Moins que ma vie martyrisés

It was her utterly inhuman
Look the scar across her neck
Came out of this pub drunk that woman
Just as I saw the final wreck
Of human love and all that's human

When at last wise Ulysses came
Back to his country and his home
His old hound remembered him
And standing by her long-worked loom
His wife awaited his return

And Sakuntala's royal mate
Weary of victories was glad
To find her pale from the long wait
And pale for love stroking her sad-
Eyed male gazelle within the gate

Of those thrice-happy kings I thought
When that false love and she whom I
Still love like shrieking harpies fought
Whose clamour darkened all the sky
And made my happiness a nought

On such regrets men found a hell
Come heaven of forgetfulness
Open to me earth's kings would sell
Their kingdoms gladly for her kiss
And their unlucky souls as well

I winter in my past come back
Bright Easter sunshine warm this heart
Chilled like towns Tamburlaine left black
And smoking pyres seen miles apart
Less martyrized than on my rack

Mon beau navire ô ma mémoire
Avons-nous assez navigué
Dans une onde mauvaise à boire
Avons-nous assez divagué
De la belle aube au triste soir

Adieu faux amour confondu
Avec la femme qui s'éloigne
Avec celle que j'ai perdue
L'année dernière en Allemagne
Et que je ne reverrai plus

Voie lactée ô sœur lumineuse
Des blancs ruisseaux de Chanaan
Et des corps blancs des amoureuses
Nageurs morts suivrons-nous d'ahan
Ton cours vers d'autres nébuleuses

Je me souviens d'une autre année
C'était l'aube d'un jour d'avril
J'ai chanté ma joie bien-aimée
Chanté l'amour à voix virile
Au moment d'amour de l'année

Oh memory my lovely ship
When will our voyaging be done
In waters dangerous to sip
As wandering from our course we run
From dawn's bright to night's filthy lip

Farewell to that false love who wore
The likeness of the woman who
Resembled her I lost before
In Germany to both of you
For I shall never see her more

O milky way bright sister to
The chalk streams of the Promised Land
And white bodies of girls in love
We follow hard hold out a hand
Lead us to farther nebulae

I remember another year
It was an April dawn I sang
My joy in her who was so dear
To me and singing my voice rang
Bells in the tender time of year

AUBADE
CHANTÉE A LÆTARE UN AN PASSÉ

C'est le printemps viens-t'en Pâquette
Te promener au bois joli
Les poules dans la cour caquètent
L'aube au ciel fait de roses plis
L'amour chemine à ta conquête

Mars et Vénus sont revenus
Ils s'embrassent à bouches folles
Devant des sites ingénus
Où sous les roses qui feuillolent
De beaux dieux roses dansent nus

Viens ma tendresse est la régente
De la floraison qui paraît
La nature est belle et touchante
Pan sifflote dans la forêt
Les grenouilles humides chantent

SONG FOR LAETARE A YEAR PAST

Here's spring again come out and see
Come and be flowers in the wood
The courtyard hens scold you and me
Dawn ruffles the grey sky with rose
Love cries who'll conquer if not he

Mars and Venus are come again
Their mouths are mad with kissing they
Lie embracing openly
Where rose-coloured dance and play
Naked gods and roses climb

Come see my love is queen of this
Flowering of all green things
Nature's all love and tenderness
And in the forest great Pan sings
The frogs are croaking their gladness

Beaucoup de ces dieux ont péri
C'est sur eux que pleurent les saules
Le grand Pan l'amour Jésus-Christ
Sont bien morts et les chats miaulent
Dans la cour je pleure à Paris

Moi qui sais des lais pour les reines
Les complaintes de mes années
Des hymnes d'esclave aux murènes
La romance du mal-aimé
Et des chansons pour les sirènes

L'amour est mort j'en suis tremblant
J'adore de belles idoles
Les souvenirs lui ressemblant
Comme la femme de Mausole
Je reste fidèle et dolent

Je suis fidèle comme un dogue
Au maître le lierre au tronc
Et les Cosaques Zaporogues
Ivrognes pieux et larrons
Aux steppes et au décalogue

Portez comme un joug le Croissant
Qu'interrogent les astrologues
Je suis le Sultan tout-puissant
O mes Cosaques Zaporogues
Votre Seigneur éblouissant

Devenez mes sujets fidèles
Leur avait écrit le Sultan
Ils rirent à cette nouvelle
Et répondirent à l'instant
A la lueur d'une chandelle

Many of those gods are dead
It is for them the willows weep
Pan Eros Jesus Christ all dead
The cats miaow I sit and weep
In Paris how the gods are dead

I who know lays fit for queens
And elegies for all my past
Dirges for slaves thrown to the eels
This song of the ill-loved and last
The sirens' chant and what it means

I tremble love is dead for I
Have worshipped idols all my life
Love's memories are like him I cry
Am plaintive as Mausolus' wife
Who wept because he had to die

And I am faithful as a dog
Or as the ivy to the oak
Or the Cossacks of Zapur-Og
Who drank and robbed in holy smoke
Of incense steppes and decalogue

My loyal Zapur-Og Cossacks
The Sultan's letter thus began
Come yoke the crescent to your backs
The mystic crescent no one can
Divine the astrologer's axe

My dazzled subjects I am yours
Omnipotently the Sultan
When they had read it there were roars
Of laughter and one of them ran
For ink and candle to their stores

RÉPONSE DES COSAQUES ZAPOROGUES
AU SULTAN DE CONSTANTINOPLE

Plus criminel que Barrabas
Cornu comme les mauvais anges
Quel Belzébuth es-tu là-bas
Nourri d'immondice et de fange
Nous n'irons pas à tes sabbats

Poisson pourri de Salonique
Long collier des sommeils affreux
D'yeux arrachés à coup de pique
Ta mère fit un pet foireux
Et tu naquis de sa colique

Bourreau de Podolie Amant
Des plaies des ulcères des croûtes
Groin de cochon cul de jument
Tes richesses garde-les toutes
Pour payer tes médicaments

REPLY OF THE ZAPUR-OG COSSACKS
TO THE SULTAN OF CONSTANTINOPLE

Worse than Bar-Abbas what beast
With devil's horns are you down there
Beelzebub at very least
Feed on your filth stay in your lair
We shall not keep your bloody feast

That stinking swollen Black Sea trout
That succubus your mother clung
Your father dreamed his eyes gouged out
And you were dropped amidst her dung
Thus were you born without a doubt

Hangman to all Podolia
Great Lover revelling in pox
Wet snout of pig black hole of mare
Hang on to your old moneybox
Smear some expensive ointment there

Voie lactée ô sœur lumineuse
Des blancs ruisseaux de Chanaan
Et des corps blancs des amoureuses
Nageurs morts suivrons-nous d'ahan
Ton cours vers d'autres nébuleuses

Regret des yeux de la putain
Et belle comme une panthère
Amour vos baisers florentins
Avaient une saveur amère
Qui a rebuté nos destins

Ses regards laissaient une traîne
D'étoiles dans les soirs tremblants
Dans ses yeux nageaient les sirènes
Et nos baisers mordus sanglants
Faisaient pleurer nos fées marraines

Mais en vérité je l'attends
Avec mon cœur avec mon âme
Et sur le pont des Reviens-t'en
Si jamais revient cette femme
Je lui dirai Je suis content

Mon cœur et ma tête se vident
Tout le ciel s'écoule par eux
O mes tonneaux des Danaldes
Comment faire pour être heureux
Comme un petit enfant candide

Je ne veux jamais l'oublier
Ma colombe ma blanche rade
O marguerite exfoliée
Mon île au loin ma Désirade
Ma rose mon giroflier

O milky way bright sister to
The chalk streams of the Promised Land
And white bodies of girls in love
We follow hard hold out a hand
Lead us to farther nebulae

I think of that sleek harlot's eyes
A panther among women placed
Ah love the Florentine surprise
Of kisses whose sharp bitter taste
Our Fates could hardly recognize

Her looks sowed stars in the pale twilight
Two sirens swam in her eyes' deep
And when we kissed with bruise and bite
Our fairy godmothers would weep
And we would make them weep all night

But really my only care
Is hoping to see her again
And if on that bridge of Despair
I see that woman's face again
I'll say to her I'm glad she's there

My head and heart are emptying
Into a sky empty of pain
O daughters of the Argive king
How to be happy once again
How is it that the children sing

I pray I never may forget
My dove my white harbour my
Daisy that's all heart and yet
White my island in the sky
Rose white and white stock dew wet

Les satyres et les pyraustes
Les égypans les feux follets
Et les destins damnés ou faustes
La corde au cou comme à Calais
Sur ma douleur quel holocauste

Douleur qui doubles les destins
La licorne et le capricorne
Mon âme et mon corps incertain
Te fuient ô bûcher divin qu'ornent
Des astres des fleurs du matin

Malheur dieu pâle aux yeux d'ivoire
Tes prêtres fous t'ont-ils paré
Tes victimes en robe noire
Ont-elles vainement pleuré
Malheur dieu qu'il ne faut pas croire

Et toi qui me suis en rampant
Dieu de mes dieux morts en automne
Tu mesures combien d'empans
J'ai droit que la terre me donne
O mon ombre ô mon vieux serpent

Au soleil parce que tu l'aimes
Je t'ai menée souviens-t'en bien
Ténébreuse épouse que j'aime
Tu es à moi en n'étant rien
O mon ombre en deuil de moi-même

L'hiver est mort tout enneigé
On a brûlé les ruches blanches
Dans les jardins et les vergers
Les oiseaux chantent sur les branches
Le printemps clair l'avril léger

And on this pain let Pan and all
His satyrs dance and marsh lights glare
And let a plague of locusts fall
And damned souls with a gallows stare
All my misery appal

Pain that adds pain to death and makes
A unicorn and capricorn
Where the soul in its body shakes
To flee the place where maids adorn
With asphodels the funeral stakes

Bad luck pale god with ivory eyes
Your mad priests have put black robes on
The innocents you victimize
And they have wept in vain and gone
But your religion is all lies

And you who follow me to make
Sure I do not exceed the span
Given to me on earth I take
Care old shadow of a man
Dead god of all my gods old snake

Remember how because I see
You love the sunshine best I've led
You here and there and home with me
My nothing-husband whom I've wed
My morning-shadow mourning me

Winter has lain in snow and died
They've burned the hives for honey in
The orchards and the robins cried
In the branches where the thin
Leaves are green with April's pride

Mort d'immortels argyraspides
La neige aux boucliers d'argent
Fuit les dendrophores livides
Du printemps cher aux pauvres gens
Qui resourient les yeux humides

Et moi j'ai le cœur aussi gros
Qu'un cul de dame damascène
O mon amour je t'aimais trop
Et maintenant j'ai trop de peine
Les sept épées hors du fourreau

Sept épées de mélancolie
Sans morfil ô claires douleurs
Sont dans mon cœur et la folie
Veut raisonner pour mon malheur
Comment voulez-vous que j'oublie

The silver armies of the snow
Have fallen to find death at last
Before the bearers of green boughs
Poor people glad that winter's past
Smile with blue and watery eyes

My heart's as heavy as hips such
As set Damascus girls apart
O my love I have loved too much
And now have too much hurt my heart
Feels seven stabs at every touch

Now the seven swords of sadness
Razor sharp and bright with pain
Are in my heart and in my madness
Reason seeks relief in vain
For how can I forget the gladness

LES SEPT ÉPÉES

La première est toute d'argent
Et son nom tremblant c'est Pâline
Sa lame un ciel d'hiver neigeant
Son destin sanglant gibeline
Vulcain mourut en la forgeant

La seconde nommée Noubosse
Est un bel arc-en-ciel joyeux
Les dieux s'en servent à leurs noces
Elle a tué trente Bé-Rieux
Et fut douée par Carabosse

La troisième bleu féminin
N'en est pas moins un chibriape
Appelé Lul de Faltenin
Ei que porte sur une nappe
L'Hermès Ernest devenu nain

La quatrième Malourène
Est un fleuve vert et doré
C'est le soir quand les riveraines
Y baignent leurs corps adorés
Et des chants de rameurs s'y traînent

La cinquième Sainte-Fabeau
C'est la plus belle des quenouilles
C'est un cyprès sur un tombeau
Où les quatre vents s'agenouillent
Et chaque nuit c'est un flambeau

THE SEVEN SWORDS

All silver is the first called by
A bright and trembling name *Paline*
Its blade a snowfilled winter sky
Its bloody quarrel Ghibelline
Forging it Vulcan learned to die

Second the rainbow-coloured gift
Of a hunchbacked fairy serves
As wedding arch to gods who lift
Over gods *Noubosse* whose curves
Cut thirty heads off in the Rift

The third is blue as milkveins are
But no less bloodthirsty for that
Lul de Faltenin stained in war
Lies on a cloth across the fiat
Palms of a giant dwarfed by a star

The fourth *Malourène* is a river
Green and gold it is the hour
When river-daughters bathe at evening
Naked as goddesses and our
Prayers are rowers' songs on the water

Fifth *Sainte Fabeau* no lovelier
Tapers a spindle than this steel
A cypress on a sepulchre
Where four winds meet at dusk and kneel
At night it is a flame of fire

La sixième métal de gloire
C'est l'ami aux si douces mains
Dont chaque matin nous sépare
Adieu voilà votre chemin
Les coqs s'épuisaient en fanfares

Et la septième s'exténue
Une femme une rose morte
Merci que le dernier venu
Sur mon amour ferme la porte
Je ne vous ai jamais connue

The sixth is forged of bravery
It is the gentle-handed one
We part with every morning see
This is your road farewell the sun
Called up the cock-crows endlessly

And the seventh sword of all
Fainting woman's flesh dead rose
Welcome then the last of all
See that on my love you close
The door we never met at all

Voie lactée ô sœur lumineuse
Des blancs ruisseaux de Chanaan
Et des corps blancs des amoureuses
Nageurs morts suivrons-nous d'ahan
Ton cours vers d'autres nébuleuses

Les démons du hasard selon
Le chant du firmament nous mènent
A sons perdus leurs violons
Font danser notre race humaine
Sur la descente à reculons

Destins destins impénétrables
Rois secoués par la folie
Et ces grelottantes étoiles
De fausses femmes dans vos lits
Aux déserts que l'histoire accable

Luitpold le vieux prince régent
Tuteur de deux royautés folles
Sanglote-t-il en y songeant
Quand vacillent les lucioles
Mouches dorées de la Saint-Jean

Près d'un château sans châtelaine
La barque aux barcarols chantants
Sur un lac blanc et sous l'haleine
Des vents qui tremblent au printemps
Voguait cygne mourant sirène

Un jour le roi dans l'eau d'argent
Se noya puis la bouche ouverte
Il s'en revint en surnageant
Sur la rive dormir inerte
Face tournée au ciel changeant

O milky way bright sister to
The chalk streams of the Promised Land
And white bodies of girls in love
We follow hard hold out a hand
Lead us to farther nebulae

The fiddles of demons of chance
In the undying song of stars
With dying falls compel us dance
Our human race pursued by Mars
Runs backward as the years advance

Impenetrable destinies
Mad kings all mad with shaking heads
The stars are shivering in the skies
False wives are shivering in your beds
In deserts choked with histories

Does the old regent Luitpold
Guardian to mad princes weep
Thinking of them drowned and cold
On summer evenings when the deep
Green shadows dance with drops of gold

No lady of the house paced on
The castle roof or sauntered by
The wide white lake windblown and wan
Where bargemen sang beneath the sky
And bark swam siren and sang swan

And when the king drowned in the silver
Water floated back to shore
With open mouth he slept his eyelids
Closed his face for evermore
Turned to the turning changing skies

Juin ton soleil ardente lyre
Brûle mes doigts endoloris
Triste et mélodieux délire
J'erre à travers mon beau Paris
Sans avoir le cœur d'y mourir

Les dimanches s'y éternisent
Et les orgues de Barbarie
Y sanglotent dans les cours grises
Les fleurs aux balcons de Paris
Penchent comme la tour de Pise

Soirs de Paris ivres du gin
Flambant de l'électricité
Les tramways feux verts sur l'échine
Musiquent au long des portées
De rails leur folie de machines

Les cafés gonflés de fumée
Crient tout l'amour de leurs tziganes
De tous leurs siphons enrhumés
De leurs garçons vêtus d'un pagne
Vers toi toi que j'ai tant aimée

Moi qui sais des lais pour les reines
Les complaintes de mes années
Des hymnes d'esclave aux murènes
La romance du mal-aimé
Et des chansons pour les sirènes

Oh burning lyre of the June sun
Burning my fingers as I go
In singing and delirium
All over Paris and find no
Place where I have the heart to die

Sundays here are ages long
The hurdy-gurdies sob within
The grey courtyards a tired song
Under balconies that lean
With flowers like towers of Pisa hung

Evenings in Paris soaked in gin
Flaming with electricity
The rocking trams have lights of green
Tramrails are bars of music they
Play with the frenzy of machines

With clouds of smoke the cafés swell
And cry the love their gipsies feel
And siphons cough and hiss to tell
White loinclothed waiters shout and reel
Towards you you I have loved so well

I who know lays fit for queens
And elegies for all my past
Dirges for slaves thrown to the eels
This song of the ill-loved and last
The sirens' chant and what it means

Les colchiques

Le pré est vénéneux mais joli en automne
Les vaches y paissant
Lentement s'empoisonnent
Le colchique couleur de cerne et de lilas
Y fleurit tes yeux sont comme cette fleur-là
Violâtres comme leur cerne et comme cet automne
Et ma vie pour tes yeux lentement s'empoisonne

Les enfants de l'école viennent avec fracas
Vêtus de hoquetons et jouant de l'harmonica
Ils cueillent les colchiques qui sont comme des mères
Filles de leurs filles et sont couleur de tes paupières
Que battent comme les fleurs battent au vent dément

Le gardien du troupeau chante tout doucement
Tandis que lentes et meuglant les vaches abandonnent
Pour toujours ce grand pré mal fleuri par l'automne

Autumn Crocuses

The meadow is poisonous but pretty in the autumn
The cows that graze there
Are slowly poisoned
Meadow-saffron the colour of lilac and of shadows
Under the eyes grows there your eyes are like those flowers
Mauve as their shadows and mauve as this autumn
And for your eyes' sake my life is slowly poisoned

Children from school come with their commotion
Dressed in smocks and playing the mouth-organ
Picking autumn crocuses which are like their mothers
Daughters of their daughters and the colour of your eyelids
Which flutter like flowers in the mad breeze blown

The cowherd sings softly to himself all alone
While slow moving lowing the cows leave behind them
Forever this great meadow ill flowered by the autumn

Annie

Sur la côte du Texas
Entre Mobile et Galveston il y a
Un grand jardin tout plein de roses
Il contient aussi une villa
Qui est une grande rose

Une femme se promène souvent
Dans le jardin toute seule
Et quand je passe sur la route bordée de tilleuls
Nous nous regardons

Comme cette femme est mennonite
Ses rosiers et ses vêtements n'ont pas de boutons
Il en manque deux à mon veston
La dame et moi suivons presque le même rite

Annie

On the coast of Texas
Between Mobile and Galveston there is
A great big garden overgrown with roses
It also contains a villa
Which is one great rose

Often a woman walks
In the garden all alone
And when I pass on the lime-tree-bordered road
We look at each other

Since this woman belongs to the Mennonite sect
Her rose trees have no buds and her clothes no buttons
There are two missing from my jacket
This lady and I are almost of the same religion

Marizibill

Dans la Haute-Rue à Cologne
Elle allait et venait le soir
Offerte à tous en tout mignonne
Puis buvait lasse des trottoirs
Très tard dans les brasseries borgnes

Elle se mettait sur la paille
Pour un maquereau roux et rose
C'était un juif il sentait l'ail
Et l'avait venant de Formose
Tirée d'un bordel de Changai

Je connais gens de toutes sortes
Ils n'égalent pas leurs destins
Indécis comme feuilles mortes
Leurs yeux sont des feux mal éteints
Leurs cœurs bougent comme leurs portes

Marizibill

In the High Street of Cologne
Evenings she came and went
Pretty enough for anyone
Then drank tired of that pavement
Late in one-eyed bars alone

Never put a farthing by
Had a redhaired rosy ponce
Jew smelt of garlic caught his eye
Coming from Formosa once
In a brothel in Shanghai

I know all kinds none are quite
Equal to their fates but doubt
Shakes them like dead leaves their bright
Eyes are fires not quite out
Hearts bang like their doors all night

Le voyageur

A Fernand Fleuret

Ouvrez-moi cette porte où je frappe en pleurant

La vie est variable aussi bien que l'Euripe

Tu regardais un banc de nuages descendre
Avec le paquebot orphelin vers les fièvres futures
Et de tous ces regrets de tous ces repentirs
        Te souviens-tu

Vagues poissons arqués fleurs surmarines
Une nuit c'était la mer
Et les fleuves s'y répandaient

Je m'en souviens je m'en souviens encore

Un soir je descendis dans une auberge triste
Auprès du Luxembourg
Dans le fond de la salle il s'envolait un Christ
Quelqu'un avait un furet
Un autre un hérisson
L'on jouait aux cartes
Et toi tu m'avais oublié

Te souviens-tu du long orphelinat des gares
Nous traversâmes des villes qui tout le jour tournaient
Et vomissaient la nuit le soleil des journées
O matelots ô femmes sombres et vous mes compagnons
        Souvenez-vous-en

Deux matelots qui ne s'étaient jamais quittés
Deux matelots qui ne s'étaient jamais parlé
Le plus jeune en mourant tomba sur le côté

The Traveller

To Fernand Fleuret

Open this door that I knock upon in tears

Life is uncertain as the tides of Euripus

You were watching a cloudbank sinking towards the horizon
With the orphaned steamboat headed for the fevers of the future
And all those regrets and those repentances
    Do you remember

Waves fishes grottoes flowers on the water
One night it was the sea
And the rivers dissolving in it

I remember these things I still remember them

One evening I went into a melancholy wine-shop
Near Luxembourg
At the back of the room there was a Christ with outstretched
  wings
Someone had a ferret
And someone else had a hedgehog
There were people playing cards
And you had forgotten me

Do you remember the long orphanage of railway stations
How we passed through towns which spun round all day long
And vomited the sunshine of the days at night
O sailors O dusky women and you my companions
    Remember these things

Two sailors who had never left each other
Two sailors who had never spoken to each other
The younger one of them dying fell on his side

O vous chers compagnons
Sonneries électriques des gares chant des moissonneuses
Traîneau d'un boucher régiment des rues sans nombre
Cavalerie des ponts nuits livides de l'alcool
Les villes que j'ai vues vivaient comme des folles

Te souviens-tu des banlieues et du troupeau plaintif des paysages

Les cyprès projetaient sous la lune leurs ombres
J'écoutais cette nuit au déclin de l'été
Un oiseau langoureux et toujours irrité
Et le bruit éternel d'un fleuve large et sombre

Mais tandis que mourants roulaient vers l'estuaire
Tous les regards tous les regards de tous les yeux
Les bords étaient déserts herbus silencieux
Et la montagne à l'autre rive était très claire

Alors sans bruit sans qu'on pût voir rien de vivant
Contre le mont passèrent des ombres vivaces
De profil ou soudain tournant leurs vagues faces
Et tenant l'ombre de leurs lances en avant

Les ombres contre le mont perpendiculaire
Grandissaient ou parfois s'abaissaient brusquement
Et ces ombres barbues pleuraient humainement
En glissant pas à pas sur la montagne claire

Qui donc reconnais-tu sur ces vieilles photographies
Te souviens-tu du jour où une abeille tomba dans le feu
C'était tu t'en souviens à la fin de l'été
Deux matelots qui ne s'étaient jamais quittés
L'aîné portait au cou une chaîne de fer
Le plus jeune mettait ses cheveux blonds en tresse

Ouvrez-moi cette porte où je frappe en pleurant

La vie est variable aussi bien que l'Euripe

O you my dear companions
Electric bells in stations song of girls harvesting
A butcher's barrow the regiment of streets without number
Cavalry of bridges livid alcoholic nights
The cities I saw lived like madwomen

Do you remember the suburbs and the doleful procession of
    landscapes

The cypresses projected their shadows under the moon
I listened last night in the dying of the summer
To the complaining and forever irritated bird
And the eternal sound of a wide dark river

But while those dying looks rolled towards the estuary
All the looks all the looks of all the eyes
The banks remained deserted grassy silent
And the mountain beyond the far bank very bright

Then without a sound with nothing living in sight
Some lifelike shadows passed between me and the mountain
In profile or suddenly turning faded faces
And carrying the ghosts of their lances in front of them

Those shadows against the perpendicular cliff
Grew tall or sometimes suddenly bent down low
And all those bearded ghosts were weeping like humans
Slipping step by step across the bright mountain

Whom do you recognize then in these old photographs
Do you remember the day a bee fell into the fire
It was you remember at the end of summer
Two sailors who had never left each other
The older one had an iron chain round his neck
The younger one was braiding his blond hair

Open this door that I knock upon in tears

Life is uncertain as the tides of Euripus

La porte

La porte de l'hôtel sourit terriblement
Qu'est-ce que cela peut me faire ô ma maman
D'être cet employé pour qui seul rien n'existe
Pi-mus couples allant dans la profonde eau triste
Anges frais débarqués à Marseille hier matin
J'entends mourir et remourir un chant lointain
Humble comme je suis qui ne suis rien qui vaille

Enfant je t'ai donné ce que j'avais travaille

The Door

The door of the hotel smiles dreadfully
What meaning mother can it have for me
To get a job and give up my existence
Pi-mus swim coupled in the deep sad distance
Cool angels landed yesterday at Marseille
I hear a far song die and die away
I who am humble who am nothing worth

Child I have given you what I had now work

La chèvre du Thibet

Les poils de cette chèvre et même
Ceux d'or pour qui prit tant de peine
Jason, ne valent rien au prix
Des cheveux dont je suis épris.

Tibetan Goat

Neither this goat's fleece nor yet
The gold one that cost dear to get
For Jason come within compare
Of my love's most lovely hair.

Le lièvre

Ne sois pas lascif et peureux
Comme le lièvre et l'amoureux.
Mais que toujours ton cerveau soit
La hase pleine qui conçoit.

Hare

Don't be a lecherous timid creature
Like the lover and the hare;
But share with hares this single feature:
Have fertility: up there.

Saltimbanques

A Louis Dumur

Dans la plaine les baladins
S'éloignent au long des jardins
Devant l'huis des auberges grises
Par les villages sans églises

Et les enfants s'en vont devant
Les autres suivent en rêvant
Chaque arbre fruitier se résigne
Quand de très loin ils lui font signe

Ils ont des poids ronds ou carrés
Des tambours des cerceaux dorés
L'ours et le singe animaux sages
Quêtent des sous sur leur passage

The Circus People

To Louis Dumur

Across the plain the circus people
Pass by the sides of market gardens
In front of the doorways of grey inns
Through many a village without a steeple

Running the children lead the way
The others follow dreamily
Each fruit tree feels resigned to see
Them wave and point from far away

They have weights both square and round
And drums and hoops all gilded bright
The bear and the monkey very polite
Begging their way bow down to the ground

L'Émigrant de Landor Road

A André Billy

Le chapeau à la main il entra du pied droit
Chez un tailleur très chic et fournisseur du roi
Ce commerçant venait de couper quelques têtes
De mannequins vêtus comme il faut qu'on se vête

La foule en tous les sens remuait en mêlant
Des ombres sans amour qui se traînaient par terre
Et des mains vers le ciel plein de lacs de lumière
S'envolaient quelquefois comme des oiseaux blancs

    Mon bateau partira demain pour l'Amérique
        Et je ne reviendrai jamais
Avec l'argent gagné dans les prairies lyriques
Guider mon ombre aveugle en ces rues que j'aimais

Car revenir c'est bon pour un soldat des Indes
Les boursiers ont vendu tous mes crachats d'or fin
Mais habillé de neuf je veux dormir enfin
Sous des arbres pleins d'oiseaux muets et de singes

Les mannequins pour lui s'étant déshabillés
Battirent leurs habits puis les lui essayèrent
Le vêtement d'un lord mort sans avoir payé
Au rabais l'habilla comme un millionnaire

        Au dehors les années
        Regardaient la vitrine
        Les mannequins victimes
        Et passaient enchaînées

Intercalées dans l'an c'étaient les journées veuves
Les vendredis sanglants et lents d'enterrements
De blancs et de tout noirs vaincus des cieux qui pleuvent
Quand la femme du diable a battu son amant

The Landor Road Emigrant

To André Billy

His hat in his hand he stepped right foot first
Into a smart and by-appointment-to-the-King tailor's
Which tradesman had just beheaded several
Dummies dressed in unexceptionable clothes

The crowd moved about in all directions mingling
Loveless shadows which dragged on the ground
And sometimes hands flew up like white birds
Towards the sky full of lakes of light

    Tomorrow my ship sails for America
        And I shall never come back
With the money I have earned on those lyrical prairies
To steer my blind shadow among these streets I used to love

Because coming back is fine for a soldier from India
But the brokers have sold all my golden gobs of medals
And I want to sleep dressed in new clothes at last
Under trees full of birds which are silent and monkeys

Having undressed for his sake those same dummies
Brushed down their suits and then tried them on him
The coat of a Lord who had died without paying his bill
Rigged him out at cut price like a millionaire

        On the outside the years
        Looked in through the window
        At the victims the dummies
        And passed by linked together

Interspersed in each year were the widowed days
The bleeding interminable Fridays of funerals
White days and days of darkness defeated by skies
Which rain when the devil's wife has been beating her lover

Puis dans un port d'automne aux feuilles indécises
Quand les mains de la foule y feuillolaient aussi
Sur le pont du vaisseau il posa sa valise
                    Et s'assit

Les vents de l'Océan en soufflant leurs menaces
Laissaient dans ses cheveux de longs baisers mouillés
Des émigrants tendaient vers le port leurs mains lasses
Et d'autres en pleurant s'étaient agenouillés

Il regarda longtemps les rives qui moururent
Seuls des bateaux d'enfant tremblaient à l'horizon
Un tout petit bouquet flottant à l'aventure
Couvrit l'Océan d'une immense floraison

Il aurait voulu ce bouquet comme la gloire
Jouer dans d'autres mers parmi tous les dauphins
            Et l'on tissait dans sa mémoire
            Une tapisserie sans fin
            Qui figurait son histoire

            Mais pour noyer changées en poux
Ces tisseuses têtues qui sans cesse interrogent
            Il se maria comme un doge
Aux cris d'une sirène moderne sans époux

Gonfle-toi vers la nuit O Mer Les yeux des squales
Jusqu'à l'aube ont guetté de loin avidement
Des cadavres de jours rongés par les étoiles
Parmi le bruit des flots et les derniers serments

Then in an autumn seaport among indecisive leaves
While the hands of the crowd were hesitating like leaves there
He put down his suitcase on the deck of the ship
              And sat down

The winds of the Ocean blustering their threats
Left their long damp kisses in his hair
Emigrants stretched out feeble hands to the quayside
While others in tears had fallen to their knees

He watched for a long time the coast disappearing
And only toy ships bobbed on the horizon
A little bunch of flowers floating at hazard
Covered the ocean with an immense flowering

He wished as one wishes for glory that these flowers
Might play in other seas among all the dolphins
              And there was woven in his memory
              An endless tapestry
              Representing his past

But those obstinate embroidresses who keep questioning
Turned into head-lice and to drown them he married
The same sea that the Doges used to marry
To the cries of a modern siren with no mate

Swell to the night O sea The eyes of the sharks
As far as the dawn have hungrily been searching
For the corpses of days gnawed into by the stars
Among the hiss of the waves and the cries of the dying

Rosemonde

A André Derain

Longtemps au pied du perron de
La maison où entra la dame
Que j'avais suivie pendant deux
Bonnes heures à Amsterdam
Mes doigts jetèrent des baisers

Mais le canal était désert
Le quai aussi et nul ne vit
Comment mes baisers retrouvèrent
Celle à qui j'ai donné ma vie
Un jour pendant plus de deux heures

Je la surnommai Rosemonde
Voulant pouvoir me rappeler
Sa bouche fleurie en Hollande
Puis lentement je m'en allai
Pour quêter la Rose du Monde

Rosemonde

To André Derain

For a long time on the step
Of the house the lady went
Into that I'd followed for
Two good hours in Amsterdam
Kisses flew up from my fingers

But the canal was empty and
So was the quayside no one saw
How my kisses followed her
To whom I'd given my whole life
For more than two long hours that day

So I named her Rosemonde
Wanting to remember her
Mouth that had flowered in Holland
Then I slowly went away
To seek the Rose of all the World

Mai

Le mai le joli mai en barque sur le Rhin
Des dames regardaient du haut de la montagne
Vous êtes si jolies mais la barque s'éloigne
Qui donc a fait pleurer les saules riverains

Or des vergers fleuris se figeaient en arrière
Les pétales tombés des cerisiers de mai
Sont les ongles de celle que j'ai tant aimée
Les pétales flétris sont comme ses paupières

Sur le chemin du bord du fleuve lentement
Un ours un singe un chien menés par des tziganes
Suivaient une roulotte traînée par un âne
Tandis que s'éloignait dans les vignes rhénanes
Sur un fifre lointain un air de régiment

Le mai le joli mai a paré les ruines
De lierre de vigne vierge et de rosiers
Le vent du Rhin secoue sur le bord les osiers
Et les roseaux jaseurs et les fleurs nues des vignes

May

In May lovely May on a boat on the Rhine
There were ladies looking from high on the mountain
You are so very pretty but the boat glides past
But who has made the willows weep on the river bank

Now the flowering orchards stood frozen astern
The petals fallen from the cherry trees in May
Are the fingernails of her whom I loved so much
And the faded petals are like her eyelids

Along the road on the river bank slowly
A bear a monkey and a dog led by gipsies
Followed a caravan pulled by a donkey
While amongst the vineyards of the Rhine valley
A regimental tune on a fife passed away

May lovely May has garlanded the ruins
With ivy Virginia creeper and wild rose
The wind of the Rhine stirs the willows on the bank
And the whispering rushes and the naked vine flowers

La synagogue

Ottomar Scholem et Abraham Loeweren
Coiffés de feutres verts le matin du sabbat
Vont à la synagogue en longeant le Rhin
Et les coteaux où les vignes rougissent là bas

Ils se disputent et crient des choses qu'on ose à peine traduire
Bâtard conçu pendant les règles ou Que le diable entre dans ton
      père
Le vieux Rhin soulève sa face ruisselante et se détourne pour
      sourire
Ottomar Scholem et Abraham Loeweren sont en colère

Parce que pendant le sabbat on ne doit pas fumer
Tandis que les chrétiens passent avec des cigares allumés
Et parce qu'Ottomar et Abraham aiment tous deux
Lia aux yeux de brebis et dont le ventre avance un peu

Pourtant tout à l'heure dans la synagogue l'un après l'autre
Ils baiseront la thora en soulevant leur beau chapeau
Parmi les feuillards de la fête des cabanes
Ottomar en chantant sourira à Abraham

Ils déchanteront sans mesure et les voix graves des hommes
Feront gémir un Léviathan au fond du Rhin comme une voix
      d'automne
Et dans la synagogue pleine de chapeaux on agitera les loulabim
Hanoten ne Kamoth bagoim tholahoth baleoumim

Synagogue

Ottomar Scholem and Abraham Löweren
In green felt bats this Shabbat morning
Are walking to the synagogue along the bank of the Rhine
Past little hills where grapes are reddening

They are quarrelling saying well almost untranslatable things
Bastard conceived on a forbidden day or The devil penetrate
    your father
The old Rhine raises its streaming face and then turns away to
    smile
Ottomar Scholem and Abraham Löweren are angry

Because smoking is not allowed on the Sabbath
And there are Christians passing by with cigars alight
And because Ottomar and Abraham both love
Leah who has sheep's eyes and a somewhat protruding stomach

Nevertheless by and by in the synagogue they will kiss
In turn the Torah scroll removing their handsome bats
And among the foliage of Succot the festival of bowers
Ottomar will smile at Abraham in the middle of singing

They will lose both time and tune and the masculine mellow
Voices will cause a Leviathan on the river-bed like the voice
    of autumn to bellow
And in the synagogue full of hats they will be shaking their
    loulavim
Hanoten ne Kamoth bagoyim tholahoth baleoumim

Les fiançailles

A Picasso

Le printemps laisse errer les fiancés parjures
Et laisse feuilloler longtemps les plumes bleues
Que secoue le cyprès où niche l'oiseau bleu

Une Madone à l'aube a pris les églantines
Elle viendra demain cueillir les giroflées
Pour mettre aux nids des colombes qu'elle destine
Au pigeon qui ce soir semblait le Paraclet

Au petit bois de citronniers s'enamourèrent
D'amour que nous aimons les dernières venues
Les villages lointains sont comme leurs paupières
Et parmi les citrons leurs cœurs sont suspendus

*

Mes amis m'ont enfin avoué leur mépris
Je buvais à pleins verres les étoiles
Un ange a exterminé pendant que je dormais
Les agneaux les pasteurs des tristes bergeries
De faux centurions emportaient le vinaigre
Et les gueux mal blessés par l'épurge dansaient
Étoiles de l'éveil je n'en connais aucune
Les becs de gaz pissaient leur flamme au clair de lune
Des croque-morts avec des bocks tintaient des glas
A la clarté des bougies tombaient vaille que vaille
Des faux cols sur des flots de jupes mal brossées
Des accouchées masquées fêtaient leurs relevailles
La ville cette nuit semblait un archipel
Des femmes demandaient l'amour et la dulie
Et sombre sombre fleuve je me rappelle
Les ombres qui passaient n'étaient jamais jolies

The Betrothal

To Picasso

The Spring invites unfaithful lovers to wander
Allows blue feathers to flutter for a long time
Shaken by cypresses where the blue bird nests

At dawn a Madonna plucked the briar roses
Tomorrow she will come and gather wallflowers
To place them in doves' nests whom she intends for
The cock pigeon that this evening seemed the Paraclete

Girls in the lemon grove the latest comers
Have fallen in love there as we others love
Blue as their eyelids are the distant hamlets
Among the lemons now their hearts are hanging

*

My friends have at last admitted they despise me
There was I drinking stars by the brimming glassful
Then while I slept an angel exterminated
The lambs and shepherds of the mournful sheepfolds
Bogus centurions snatched away the vinegar
And beggars bruised and scratched by spurge were dancing
Stars of awakening not one was known to me
The gas jets pissed their flames out in the moonlight
Undertakers with beer glasses tolled bells
In candlelight for better or for worse
Stiff collars fell on waves of dusty skirts
Masked women in labour celebrated their churchings
That night the city seemed an archipelago
Women were asking for love and proper devotion
And sombre sombre river I remember
The shadows which passed by were never pretty

*

Je n'ai plus même pitié de moi
Et ne puis exprimer mon tourment de silence
Tous les mots que j'avais à dire se sont changés en étoiles
Un Icare tente de s'élever jusqu'à chacun de mes yeux
Et porteur de soleils je brûle au centre de deux nébuleuses
Qu'ai-je fait aux bêtes théologales de l'intelligence
Jadis les morts sont revenus pour m'adorer
Et j'espérais la fin du monde
Mais la mienne arrive en sifflant comme un ouragan

*

J'ai eu le courage de regarder en arrière
Les cadavres de mes jours
Marquent ma route et je les pleure
Les uns pourrissent dans les églises italiennes
Ou bien dans de petits bois de citronniers
Qui fleurissent et fructifient
En même temps et en toute saison
D'autres jours ont pleuré avant de mourir dans des tavernes
Où d'ardents bouquets rouaient
Aux yeux d'une mulâtresse qui inventait la poésie
Et les roses de l'électricité s'ouvrent encore
Dans le jardin de ma mémoire

*

I no longer even have pity for myself
And cannot express the torture of this silence
All the words which I once had to say have been changed into
    stars
There is an Icarus trying to force his way up as far as my eyes
And bearer of suns I am burning between two nebulae
What have I done to the theological beasts of the intelligence
Once the dead used to return to worship me
And I looked forward to the end of the world
But now my own is coming towards me hissing like a hurricane

*

I have summoned up the courage to look back
The corpses of my days
Litter my path and I mourn them
Some of them are rotting in Italian churches
Or else in little lemon groves
Flowering and giving fruit
At the same time and in all seasons
Other days wept before they died in drinking places
Where burning flowers fanned out
In the eyes of a half-caste woman who invented poetry
And the roses of the electricity still bloom
In the garden of my memory

*

Pardonnez-moi mon ignorance
Pardonnez-moi de ne plus connaître l'ancien jeu des vers
Je ne sais plus rien et j'aime uniquement
Les fleurs à mes yeux redeviennent des flammes
Je médite divinement
Et je souris des êtres que je n'ai pas créés
Mais si le temps venait où l'ombre enfin solide
Se multipliait en réalisant la diversité formelle de mon amour
J'admirerais mon ouvrage

*

J'observe le repos du dimanche
Et je loue la paresse
Comment comment réduire
L'infiniment petite science
Que m'imposent mes sens
L'un est pareil aux montagnes au ciel
Aux villes à mon amour
Il ressemble aux saisons
Il vit décapité sa tête est le soleil
Et la lune son cou tranché
Je voudrais éprouver une ardeur infinie
Monstre de mon ouïe tu rugis et tu pleures
Le tonnerre te sert de chevelure
Et tes griffes répètent le chant des oiseaux
Le toucher monstrueux m'a pénétré m'empoisonne
Mes yeux nagent loin de moi
Et les astres intacts sont mes maîtres sans épreuve
La bête des fumées a la tête fleurie
Et le monstre le plus beau
Ayant la saveur du laurier se désole

*

Forgive me for my ignorance
Forgive me for no longer knowing the old game of verse
I know nothing any more I only love
In my eyes flowers become flames again
I meditate divinely
And smile on beings I have not created
But if the time came when shadow at last solid
Multiplied itself in order to realize the formal diversity of my love
I should admire my work

I observe the Sunday rest
And I praise laziness
How but how distil
The infinitesimal knowledge
Imposed on me by my senses
One of which is like the mountains of the sky
And the cities of my love
It resembles the seasons
It is alive though headless its head is the sun
And the moon its severed neck
I wish I could experience an infinite ardour
Monster of my hearing you are roaring and weeping
You have the thunder for hair
And your claws repeat the shrillness of the birds
The monstrous sense of touch invades and poisons me
My eyes swim far off from me
And the pure stars are my untried masters
The beast of the smokes and fogs has a blossoming head
And the most beautiful beast of all
Catches the scent of bay leaves and is desolate

A la fin les mensonges ne me font plus peur
C'est la lune qui cuit comme un œuf sur le plat
Ce collier de gouttes d'eau va parer la noyée
Voici mon bouquet de fleurs de la Passion
Qui offrent tendrement deux couronnes d'épines
Les rues sont mouillées de la pluie de naguère
Des anges diligents travaillent pour moi à la maison
La lune et la tristesse disparaîtront pendant
Toute la sainte journée
Toute la sainte journée j'ai marché en chantant
Une dame penchée à sa fenêtre m'a regardé longtemps
M'éloigner en chantant

*

Au tournant d'une rue je vis des matelots
Qui dansaient le cou nu au son d'un accordéon
J'ai tout donné au soleil
Tout sauf mon ombre

Les dragues les ballots les sirènes mi-mortes
A l'horizon brumeux s'enfonçaient les trois-mâts
Les vents ont expiré couronnés d'anémones
O Vierge signe pur du troisième mois

*

In the end lies no longer frighten me
There is the moon cooking like a fried egg
This necklace of water-drops is for the drowned girl
And here is my bouquet of Passion flowers
Which put forth tenderly two crowns of thorns
The streets are wet with the rain of not long since
Diligent angels are at work in my house
The moon and sorrow will be disappearing
All the holy day
All the holy day I have walked and sung
A lady leaning from her window watched me a long time
As I walked away singing

*

At the corner of a street I saw some sailors dancing
With turned-down collars to the sound of an accordion
I have given to the sun
Everything except my shadow

Dredgers bales on quaysides half-drowned sirens
Three-masters melted on the dim horizon
The winds expired their wreaths were windflowers
O Virgin pure sign of the third House

*

Templiers flamboyants je brûle parmi vous
Prophétisons ensemble ô grand maître je suis
Le désirable feu qui pour vous se dévoue
Et la girande tourne ô belle ô belle nuit

Liens déliés par une libre flamme Ardeur
Que mon souffle éteindra O Morts à quarantaine
Je mire de ma mort la gloire et le malheur
Comme si je visais l'oiseau de la quintaine

Incertitude oiseau feint peint quand vous tombiez
Le soleil et l'amour dansaient dans le village
Et tes enfants galants bien ou mal habillés
Ont bâti ce bûcher le nid de mon courage

*

O flaming Templars I am burning in your midst
Now let us prophesy Grand Master I am the bright
Desirable fire which burns at your august behest
And the great wheel of fire turns burns oh beauteous night

The bonds are loosened by a liberating flame
Burning my breath will quench O Dead in lenten dark
I see my own death's pain and glory and take aim
As sure as if I tilted at a bird for mark

Indecision bird feigned painted when you fell
The sun and also love were dancing in the village
And your gay gaudy children poorly dressed or well
Piled up this heap of sticks this nest to hatch my courage

1909

La dame avait une robe
En ottoman violine
Et sa tunique brodée d'or
Était composée de deux panneaux
S'attachant sur l'épaule

Les yeux dansants comme des anges
Elle riait elle riait
Elle avait un visage aux couleurs de France
Les yeux bleus les dents blanches et les lèvres très rouges
Elle avait un visage aux couleurs de France

Elle était décolletée en rond
Et coiffée à la Récamier
Avec de beaux bras nus

N'entendra-t-on jamais sonner minuit

La dame en robe d'ottoman violine
Et en tunique brodée d'or
Décolletée en rond
Promenait ses boucles
Son bandeau d'or
Et traînait ses petits souliers à boucles

Elle était si belle
Que tu n'aurais pas osé l'aimer

J'aimais les femmes atroces dans les quartiers énormes
Où naissaient chaque jour quelques êtres nouveaux
Le fer était leur sang la flamme leur cerveau
J'aimais j'aimais le peuple habile des machines
Le luxe et la beauté ne sont que son écume
Cette femme était si belle
Qu'elle me faisait peur

1909

The lady had a dress
Of violet-coloured silk
And her gold-embroidered tunic
Was made up of two panels
Fastened at the shoulder

Her eyes dancing like angels
She laughed she laughed
She had a face which was all the colours of France
Her eyes blue her teeth white her lips very red
She had a face which was all the colours of France

Her dress had a round neck
Her hair was done like Récamier's
Her arms were beautiful and bare

Shall we never hear midnight strike

The lady in the violet-coloured silk dress
And the gold-embroidered tunic
With the round neckline
Walked with her ringlets
And her gold bandeau
Trailing her little buckled shoes

She was so beautiful
You would not have dared to love her

I used to love frightful women in enormous districts
Where every day several new beings are born
Iron was their blood flame was their brain
I loved the common people clever with machinery
Luxury and beauty are only its froth
That woman was so beautiful
She frightened me

A la Santé

I

Avant d'entrer dans ma cellule
Il a fallu me mettre nu
Et quelle voix sinistre ulule
Guillaume qu'es-tu devenu

Le Lazare entrant dans la tombe
Au lieu d'en sortir comme il fit
Adieu adieu chantante ronde
O mes années ô jeunes filles

Non je ne me sens plus là
      Moi-même
Je suis le quinze de la
      Onzième

Le soleil filtre à travers
      Les vitres
Ses rayons font sur mes vers
      Les pitres

Et dansent sur le papier
      J'écoute
Quelqu'un qui frappe du pied
      La voûte

In the Santé

I

Before I got into my cell
I had to strip my body bare
I heard an ominous voice say Well
Guillaume what are you doing here

Lazarus steps into the ground
Not out of it as he was bid
Adieu adieu O singing round
Of years and girls the life I led

II

I'm no longer myself in here
        I know
I'm number fifteen in the eleventh
        Row

The sunlight filters downward through
        The panes
And on these lines bright clowns alight
        Like stains

They dance under my eyes while my
        Ears follow
The feet of one whose feet above
        Sound hollow

III

Dans une fosse comme un ours
Chaque matin je me promène
Tournons tournons tournons toujours
Le ciel est bleu comme une chaîne
Dans une fosse comme un ours
Chaque matin je me promène

Dans la cellule d'à côté
On y fait couler la fontaine
Avec les clefs qu'il fait tinter
Que le geôlier aille et revienne
Dans la cellule d'à côté
On y fait couler la fontaine

IV

Que je m'ennuie entre ces murs tout nus
    Et peints de couleurs pâles
Une mouche sur le papier à pas menus
    Parcourt mes lignes inégales

Que deviendrai-je ô Dieu qui connais ma douleur
    Toi qui me l'as donnée
Prends en pitié mes yeux sans larmes ma pâleur
    Le bruit de ma chaise enchaînée

Et tous ces pauvres cœurs battant dans la prison
    L'Amour qui m'accompagne
Prends en pitié surtout ma débile raison
    Et ce désespoir qui la gagne

III

In a bear-pit like a bear
Every morning round I tramp
Round and round and round and round
The sky is like an iron clamp
In a bear-pit like a bear
Every morning round I tramp

In the next cell at the sink
Someone lets the water run
With his bunch of keys that clink
Let the gaoler go and come
In the next cell at the sink
Someone lets the water run

IV

How bored I am between bare wall and wall
        Whose colour pales and pines
A fly on the paper with extremely small
        Steps runs across these lines

What will become of me O God Who know
        My pain Who gave it me
Have pity on my dry eyes and my pallor
        My chair which creaks and is not free

And all these poor hearts beating in this prison
        And Love beside me seated
Pity above all my unstable reason
        And this despair which threatens to defeat it

V

Que lentement passent les heures
Comme passe un enterrement

Tu pleureras l'heure où tu pleures
Qui passera trop vitement
Comme passent toutes les heures

VI

J'écoute les bruits de la ville
Et prisonnier sans horizon
Je ne vois rien qu'un ciel hostile
Et les murs nus de ma prison

Le jour s'en va voici que brûle
Une lampe dans la prison
Nous sommes seuls dans ma cellule
Belle clarté Chère raison

Septembre 1911

V

How long these hours take to go
As long as a whole funeral

You'll mourn the time you mourned you know
It will be gone too soon like all
Time past
            too fast too long ago

VI

I hear the noises of the city
In the turning world beyond me
I see a sky which has no pity
And bare prison walls around me

The daylight disappears and now
A lamp is lit within the prison
We're all alone here in my cell
Beautiful light Beloved reason

September 1911

Le lapin

Je connais un autre connin
Que tout vivant je voudrais prendre.
Sa garenne est parmi le thym
Des vallons du pays de Tendre.

Rabbit

There's another little cove
I'd catch living in my hand
His burrow is among the mauve
Hillocks of the Tender Land.

Le dromadaire

Avec ses quatre dromadaires
Don Pedro d'Alfaroubeira
Courut le monde et l'admira.
Il fit ce que je voudrais faire
Si j'avais quatre dromadaires.

Dromedary

Four dromedaries carried you
Don Pedro d'Alfaroubeira
Round the great world with Oh and Ah.
What you did is what I should do
Had I four dromedaries too.

Cors de chasse

Notre histoire est noble et tragique
Comme le masque d'un tyran
Nul drame hasardeux ou magique
Aucun détail indifférent
Ne rend notre amour pathétique

Et Thomas de Quincey buvant
L'opium poison doux et chaste
A sa pauvre Anne allait rêvant
Passons passons puisque tout passe
Je me retournerai souvent

Les souvenirs sont cors de chasse
Dont meurt le bruit parmi le vent

Hunting Horns

Our past is as noble and as tragic
As the mask of a tyrant
No tale of danger or of magic
Nothing so insignificant
Describes the pathos of our love

And Thomas de Quincey drinking his
Sweet and chaste and poisoned glass
Dreaming went to see his Ann
Let us since all passes pass
I shall look back only too often

Memories are hunting horns
Whose sound dies among the wind

Les fenêtres

Du rouge au vert toute le jaune se meurt
Quand chantent les aras dans les forêts natales
Abatis de pihis
Il y a un poème à faire sur l'oiseau qui n'a qu'une aile
Nous l'enverrons en message téléphonique
Traumatisme géant
Il fait couler les yeux
Voilà une jolie jeune fille parmi les jeunes Turinaises
Le pauvre jeune homme se mouchait dans sa cravate blanche
Tu soulèveras le rideau
Et maintenant voilà que s'ouvre la fenêtre
Araignées quand les mains tissaient la lumière
Beauté pâleur insondables violets
Nous tenterons en vain de prendre du repos
On commencera à minuit
Quand on a le temps on a la liberté
Bigorneaux Lotte multiples Soleils et l'Oursin du couchant
Une vieille paire de chaussures jaunes devant la fenêtre
Tours
Les Tours ce sont les rues
Puits
Puits ce sont les places
Puits
Arbres creux qui abritent les Câpresses vagabondes
Les Chabins chantent des airs à mourir
Aux Chabines marronnes
Et l'oie oua-oua trompette au nord
Où les chasseurs de ratons
Raclent les pelleteries
Étincelant diamant
Vancouver
Où le train blanc de neige et de feux nocturnes fuit l'hiver

The Windows

From the red to the green all the yellow dies
When the macaws are calling in their native forests
Slaughter of pi-his
There is a poem to be written about the bird which has only one
    wing
We had better send it in the form of a telephone message
Gigantic state of trauma
It makes your eyes water
Look there is a pretty girl among the young girls of Turin
The unfortunate young man dabbed at his eyes with his white tie
Raise the blind
And now see how the window opens
If hands could weave light this was done by spiders
Beauty pallor unfathomable indigos
We shall try in vain to rest ourselves
It is due to begin at midnight
When you have time you have freedom
Winkles Eel-pout multiplied Suns and the Sea-urchin of the sunset
An old pair of yellow shoes under the window
Towers
Towers are streets
Wells
Wells are squares
Wells
Hollow trees sheltering wandering black quadroon girls
The long-horned long-haired rams call dying with love
To the long-haired ewes that have strayed and are wild again
And the goose calls trumpeting in the north lands
Where the raccoon hunters
Scrape raccoon skins
Sparkling diamond
Vancouver
Where the train white with the snow and nocturnal lights
    escapes from the winter

O Paris
Du rouge au vert tout le jaune se meurt
Paris Vancouver Hyères Maintenon New-York et les Antilles
La fenêtre s'ouvre comme une orange
Le beau fruit de la lumière

O Paris
From the red to the green all the yellow dies
Paris Vancouver Hyères Maintenon New York and the West Indies
The window opens like an orange
The beautiful fruit of light

Lundi rue Christine

La mère de la concierge et la concierge laisseront tout passer
Si tu es un homme tu m'accompagneras ce soir
Il suffirait qu'un type maintînt la porte cochère
Pendant que l'autre monterait

Trois becs de gaz allumés
La patronne est poitrinaire
Quand tu auras fini nous jouerons une partie de jacquet
Un chef d'orchestre qui a mal à la gorge
Quand tu viendras à Tunis je te ferai fumer du kief

Ça a l'air de rimer

Des piles de soucoupes des fleurs un calendrier
Pim pam pim
Je dois fiche près de 300 francs à ma probloque
Je préférerais me couper le parfaitement que de les lui donner

Je partirai à 20 h. 27
Six glaces s'y dévisagent toujours
Je crois que nous allons nous embrouiller encore davantage
Cher monsieur
Vous êtes un mec à la mie de pain
Cette dame a le nez comme un ver solitaire
Louise a oublié sa fourrure
Moi je n'ai pas de fourrure et je n'ai pas froid
Le Danois fume sa cigarette en consultant l'horaire
Le chat noir traverse la brasserie

Ces crêpes étaient exquises
La fontaine coule
Robe noire comme ses ongles
C'est complètement impossible

Rue Christine Monday

The caretaker's mother and the caretaker herself will let
    anything in
If you're a man you will come with me tonight
All that would be needed would be for one bloke to keep the
    wicket gate
While the other one went up

Three gas-jets burning
The proprietress has trouble with her breathing
When you've finished we'll have a game of backgammon
An orchestral conductor with a sore throat
When you come to Tunis I'll show you how to smoke hashish

That seems to make sense

Piles of saucers some flowers a calendar
Clink clank clink
I owe blast it nearly 300 francs to my landlady
I'd rather cut off my absolutely than give her the money

I'm leaving at 8.27 p.m.
Six mirrors there still staring at each other
I'm afraid we are going to get even more mixed up
My dear Sir
You are a worthless rascal
That lady has a nose like a tapeworm
Louise has left her fur behind
As for me I haven't got a fur and I don't feel cold
The Dane is smoking his cigarette and looking at the timetable
The black cat is walking across the floor of the café

Those pancakes were delicious
The tap is running
A dress as black as her nails
It's absolutely impossible

Voici monsieur
La bague en malachite
Le sol est semé de sciure
Alors c'est vrai
La serveuse rousse a été enlevée par un libraire

Un journaliste que je connais d'ailleurs très vaguement

Écoute Jacques c'est très sérieux ce que je vais te dire

Compagnie de navigation mixte

Il me dit monsieur voulez-vous voir ce que je peux faire d'eaux
      fortes et de tableaux
Je n'ai qu'une petite bonne

Après déjeuner café du Luxembourg
Une fois là il me présente un gros bonhomme
Qui me dit
Écoutez c'est charmant
A Smyrne à Naples en Tunisie
Mais nom de Dieu où est-ce
La dernière fois que j'ai été en Chine
C'est il y a huit ou neuf ans
L'Honneur tient souvent à l'heure que marque la pendule
La quinte major

Look Sir
The malachite ring
The ground is covered with sawdust
So it's true
The redhaired waitress was abducted by a bookseller

A journalist whom by the way I know only very vaguely

Listen Jacques I'm going to tell you something very serious

Goods and passenger steam navigation company

He said to me Sir would you like to see what I can do in the way
   of etchings and paintings
All I have got is a little maid

After lunch at the Café du Luxembourg
When we got there he introduced me to a great fat fellow
Who said to me
Listen isn't it delightful
In Smyrna in Naples in Tunisia
But where was it for God's sake
The last time I was in China
That's eight or nine years ago
Honour often depends on what the clock says
The major fifth

Cœur couronne et miroir

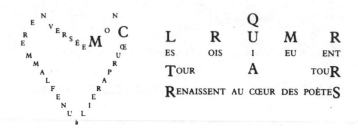

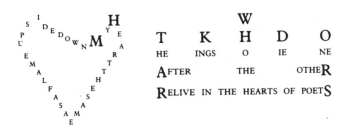

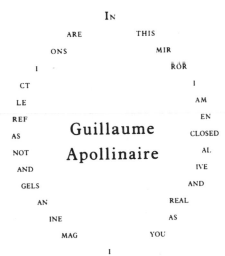

Guillaume Apollinaire

Il pleut

il pleut des voix de femmes comme si elles étaient mortes même dans le souvenir

c'est vous aussi qu'il pleut merveilleuses rencontres de ma vie ô gouttelettes

et ces nuages cabrés se prennent à hennir tout un univers de villes auriculaires

écoute s'il pleut tandis que le regret et le dédain pleurent une ancienne musique

écoute tomber les liens qui te retiennent en haut et en bas

It's Raining

it is raining women's voices as if they were dead even in memory

you also are raining down marvellous encounters of my life o little drops

and these rearing clouds are beginning to whinny a whole world of auricular towns

listen to it rain while regret and disdain weep an old fashioned music

listen to the fall of all the perpendiculars of your existence

La petite auto

Le 31 du mois d'Août 1914
Je partis de Deauville un peu avant minuit
Dans la petite auto de Rouveyre

Avec son chauffeur nous étions trois

Nous dîmes adieu à toute une époque
Des géants furieux se dressaient sur l'Europe
Les aigles quittaient leur aire attendant le soleil
Les poissons voraces montaient des abîmes
Les peuples accouraient pour se connaître à fond
Les morts tremblaient de peur dans leurs sombres demeures

Les chiens aboyaient vers là-bas où étaient les frontières
Je m'en allais portant en moi toutes ces armées qui se battaient
Je les sentais monter en moi et s'étaler les contrées où elles
      serpentaient
Avec les forêts les villages heureux de la Belgique
Francorchamps avec l'Eau Rouge et les pouhons
Région par où se font toujours les invasions
Artères ferroviaires où ceux qui s'en allaient mourir
Saluaient encore une fois la vie colorée
Océans profonds où remuaient les monstres
Dans les vieilles carcasses naufragées
Hauteurs inimaginables où l'homme combat
Plus haut que l'aigle ne plane
L'homme y combat contre l'homme
Et descend tout à coup comme une étoile filante
Je sentais en moi des êtres neufs pleins de dextérité
Bâtir et aussi agencer un univers nouveau
Un marchand d'une opulence inouïe et d'une taille prodigieuse
Disposait un étalage extraordinaire
Et des bergers gigantesques menaient

The Little Car

On the 31st day of August in the year 1914
I left Deauville shortly before midnight
In Rouveyre's little car

Including his chauffeur there were three of us

We said goodbye to a whole epoch
Furious giants were looming over Europe
The eagles were leaving their eyries expecting the sun
Voracious fishes were swimming up from the abysses
Nations were rushing together to know each other through and
    through
The dead were trembling with fear in their dark dwellings

The dogs were barking in the direction of the frontiers
As I went I carried within me all the armies that were fighting
I felt them rising within me and spreading out over the regions
    through which their columns wound
With the forests the happy villages of Belgium
Francorchamps and Eau Rouge and the *pouhons*
A region through which invasions are always taking place
And the railway arteries along which those who were going away
    to die
Saluted one more time a life full of colours
The deep oceans where monsters were stirring
In old carcasses of wrecks
The unimaginable heights where men fight
Higher than the eagle soars
Man fights there against man
And falls suddenly like a shooting star
I felt within me new beings full of dexterity
Building a new universe and running it as well
A merchant of unheard-of opulence and of prodigious stature
Was setting out an extraordinary display of stock
And gigantic shepherds were driving forward

De grands troupeaux muets qui broutaient les paroles
Et contre lesquels aboyaient tous les chiens sur la route

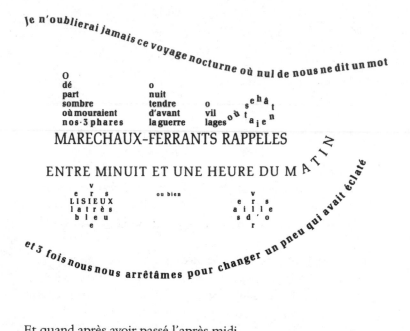

Et quand après avoir passé l'après-midi
Par Fontaînebleau
Nous arrivâmes à Paris
Au moment où l'on affichait la mobilisation
Nous comprîmes mon camarade et moi
Que la petite auto nous avait conduits dans une époque
                    Nouvelle
Et bien qu'étant déjà tous deux des hommes mûrs
Nous venions cependant de naître

Great dumb flocks grazing on words as they went
And at them barked all the dogs along the road

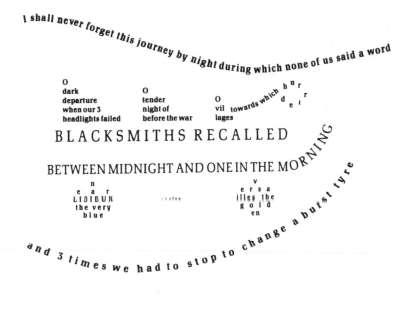

I shall never forget this journey by night during which none of us said a word

O
dark   O
departure   tender   O
when our 3   night of   vil towards which h a r
headlights failed before the war lages   d e i r

BLACKSMITHS RECALLED

BETWEEN MIDNIGHT AND ONE IN THE MORNING
        n   v
    e   a   r   e r s a
    LIBIBUN   illes the
    the very   g o l d
      blue   en

and 3 times we had to stop to change a burst tyre

And when having passed through Fontainebleau
During the afternoon
We got to Paris
At the moment at which the mobilization posters were going up
We understood my comrade and I
That the little car had brought us into a new
                    Era
And that although we were both already fully grown men
We had nevertheless just been born

Fête

A André Rouveyre

Feu d'artifice en acier
Qu'il est charmant cet éclairage
   Artifice d'artificier
Mêler quelque grâce au courage

Deux fusants
Rose éclatement
Comme deux seins que l'on dégrafe
Tendent leurs bouts insolemment
IL SUT AIMER
      quelle épitaphe

Un poète dans la forêt
Regarde avec indifférence
   Son revolver au cran d'arrêt
Des roses mourir d'espérance

Il songe aux roses de Saadi
Et soudain sa tête se penche
Car une rose lui redit
La molle courbe d'une hanche

L'air est plein d'un terrible alcool
Filtré des étoiles mi-closes
Les obus caressent le mol
Parfum nocturne où tu reposes
    Mortification des roses

Gala

To André Rouveyre

Skyrocket burst of hardened steel
A charming light on this fair place
These technicians' tricks appeal
Mixing with courage a little grace

Two star shells first
In rose pink burst
Two breasts you lay bare with a laugh
Offer their insolent tips
                HERE LIES
ONE WHO COULD LOVE
                    some epitaph

A poet in the forest sees
Indifferent able to cope
His revolver catch at safe
Roses dying of their hope

Thinks of Saadi's roses then
Bows his head draws down his lip
As a rose reminds him of
The softer curving of a hip

The air is full of a terrible
Liquor from half-shut stars distilled
Projectiles stroke the soft nocturnal
Perfume with your image filled
        Where the roses all are killed

Exercice

Vers un village de l'arrière
S'en allaient quatre bombardiers
Ils étaient couverts de poussière
Depuis la tête jusqu'aux pieds

Ils regardaient la vaste plaine
En parlant entre eux du passé
Et ne se retournaient qu'à peine
Quand un obus avait toussé

Tous quatre de la classe seize
Parlaient d'antan non d'avenir
Ainsi se prolongeait l'ascèse
Qui les exerçait à mourir

Exercise

Towards a village in the rear
Four artillerymen were walking
Covered with dust from ruffled hair
To dusty boots and slowly talking

Looking at the immensity
Of flatness talking of the past
And hardly turning round to see
Where a shell had coughed from last

All four Class of 1916
Reminiscing not prophesying
Prolonging the ascetic life
Of those who are rehearsing dying

Carte postale

Je t'écris de dessous la tente
Tandis que meurt ce jour d'été
Où floraison éblouissante
Dans le ciel à peine bleuté
Une canonnade éclatante
Se fane avant d'avoir été

Postcard

(Sent to André Rouveyre, 20 August 1915)

I write to you beneath this tent
While summer day becomes a shade
And startling magnificent
Flowers of the cannonade
Stud the pale blue firmament
And before existing fade

La souris

Belles journées, souris du temps,
Vous rongez peu à peu ma vie.
Dieu! Je vais avoir vingt-huit ans,
Et mal vécus, à mon envie.

Mouse

Beautiful days, time's mice, gnawing
Little by little my life away.
God! Nearly twenty-eight this spring,
And misspent years too, I should say.

La carpe

Dans vos viviers, dans vos étangs,
Carpes, que vous vivez longtemps!
Est-ce que la mort vous oublie,
Poissons de la mélancolie.

Carp

In your fish-pools and your ponds
O carp, how your lives are long!
Does death forget that you're his dish,
O most melancholy fish?

La jolie rousse

Me voici devant tous un homme plein de sens
Connaissant la vie et de la mort ce qu'un vivant peut connaître
Ayant éprouvé les douleurs et les joies de l'amour
Ayant su quelquefois imposer ses idées
Connaissant plusieurs langages
Ayant pas mal voyagé
Ayant vu la guerre dans l'Artillerie et l'Infanterie
Blessé à la tête trépané sous le chloroforme
Ayant perdu ses meilleurs amis dans l'effroyable lutte
Je sais d'ancien et de nouveau autant qu'un homme seul pourrait
     des deux savoir
Et sans m'inquiéter aujourd'hui de cette guerre
Entre nous et pour nous mes amis
Je juge cette longue querelle de la tradition et de l'invention
       De l'Ordre et de l'Aventure

Vous dont la bouche est faite à l'image de celle de Dieu
Bouche qui est l'ordre même
Soyez indulgents quand vous nous comparez
A ceux qui furent la perfection de l'ordre
Nous qui quêtons partout l'aventure

Nous ne sommes pas vos ennemis
Nous voulons vous donner de vastes et d'étranges domaines
Où le mystère en fleurs s'offre à qui veut le cueillir
Il y a là des feux nouveaux des couleurs jamais vues
Mille phantasmes impondérables
Auxquels il faut donner de la réalité

Nous voulons explorer la bonté contrée énorme où tout se tait
Il y a aussi le temps qu'on peut chasser ou faire revenir

The Pretty Red-Head

Here I stand before everyone a man full of sense
One who understands life and of death as much as a living
    person can understand
One who has suffered the pains and joys of love
One who has sometimes succeeded in convincing others
One who is acquainted with several languages
One who has travelled more than a little
One who has seen war both in the Artillery and the Infantry
One who has been wounded in the head and trepanned under
    chloroform
One who has lost his best friends in the terrible slaughter
I know as much about what is old and what is new as a single
    person could know
And without troubling now about this war
Between ourselves and for our own sakes my friends
I sit in judgement on this long quarrel between tradition and
    invention
               Between Order and Adventure

You whose mouths are fashioned in the image of God's mouth
Mouth which is order itself
Be lenient when you compare us
With those who were perfect order
Us who seek adventure everywhere

We are not your enemies
We want to bequeath to you vast and strange domains
Where the flower of mystery offers itself to anyone who wishes
    to pluck it
There there are unknown fires and colours never before seen
A thousand unknowable phantasms
Which must be given reality

We wish to explore kindness the vast and peaceful country
There is also Time which can either be banished or else retrieved

Pitié pour nous qui combattons toujours aux frontières
De l'illimité et de l'avenir
Pitié pour nos erreurs pitié pour nos péchés

Voici que vient l'été la saison violente
Et ma jeunesse est morte ainsi que le printemps
O Soleil c'est le temps de la Raison ardente
                    Et j'attends
Pour la suivre toujours la forme noble et douce
Qu'elle prend afin que je l'aime seulement
Elle vient et m'attire ainsi qu'un fer l'aimant
                Elle a l'aspect charmant
                D'une adorable rousse

Ses cheveux sont d'or on dirait
Un bel éclair qui durerait
Ou ces flammes qui se pavanent
Dans les roses-thé qui se fanent

Mais riez riez de moi
Hommes de partout surtout gens d'ici
Car il y a tant de choses que je n'ose vous dire
Tant de choses que vous ne me laisseriez pas dire
Ayez pitié de moi

Pity on us who are always fighting at the frontiers
Of limitlessness and the future
Pity for our mistakes pity for our sins

Here comes the summer now the violent season
My youth lies dead as springtime it is late
O sun this is the hour of burning Reason
                    And I await
In order to follow it always the sweet form
And noble she will take that everywhere
And only I shall love She comes and draws me
          She has the look of a lovely
          Girl with redgold hair

Her hair is gold it is so bright
Like a lasting flash of light
Or like the flames which slow parade
In tea-roses as they fade

But laugh at me go on laugh
Men everywhere and especially people here
There are so many things I do not dare to tell you
So many things you would not let me tell you
Have pity on me

Bleuet

Jeune homme
de vingt ans
Qui as vu des choses si affreuses
Que penses-tu des hommes de ton enfance

Tu   Tu
    as
        vu   connais
        la
            mort   la bravoure et la ruse
                en
                    face
                        plus
                            de
                                cent
                                    fois
                                        tu
                                            ne
                                                sais
Transmets ton intrépidité   pas
                                                    ce
A ceux qui viendront   que
                                                            c'est
            Après toi   que
                                                                    la
                                                                    vie

        Jeune homme
    Tu es joyeux ta mémoire est ensanglantée
            Ton âme est rouge aussi
                De joie
Tu as absorbé la vie de ceux qui sont morts près de toi
            Tu as de la décision
        Il est 17 heures et tu saurais

Cornflower

Young man
of twenty
Who have seen such terrible things
What do you think of the grown men of your childhood

You   You

have

seen   know

death

face   bravery and cunning

to

face

more

than

a

hundred

times

you

do

Communicate your fearlessness   not

know

To those who will come   what

life

After you   is

Young man
You are full of joy your memory is full of blood
Your soul is also red
With joy
You have absorbed the life of those who died close to you
You have the quality of decision
It is 1700 hrs and you would know how to

Mourir
Sinon mieux que tes aînés
    Du moins plus pieusement
    Car tu connais mieux la mort que la vie
    O douceur d'autrefois
        Lenteur immémoriale

Die
If no better than your elders
    At least more piously
    For you know death better than life
    O sweetness of other times
        Immemorial slowness

Le jupon

Bonjour Germaine Vous avez un beau jupon
Un beau jupon de reine et de reine cruelle
Que j'en tâte la soie Une soie du Japon
Qu'orne un large volant d'ancienne dentelle

Cette cloche de soie où le double battant
De vos jambes tinta le glas de mes caprices
J'en sonne ma Germaine le sein haletant
Et les mains appuyées sur vos hanches complices

Votre chambre ma cloche est un charmant clocher
Où mes mains sur la soie déchirent mes oreilles
Les patères gibet des jupons accrochés
Balancent des pendus soyeux qui m'émerveillent

Immobile comme un hibou la lampe veille

The Skirt

Hallo Germaine that's a fine skirt you have
A fine skirt for a queen A cruel queen
Let's feel the silk of it Silk from Japan
And trimmed with wide lace made on no machine

Your skirt's a silken bell whose double clapper
Your legs have struck the passing of my fancies
O Germaine now I ring it my breast heaving
My hands press down upon your willing haunches

Your bedroom O my bell is a fine belfry
My hands touch silk and seem to tear my ears
Those pegs are gallows on which skirts are hanging
Those hanging men are dazzling my eyes

Motionless as an owl the oil lamp watches

Prière

Quand j'étais un petit enfant
Ma mère ne m'habillait que de bleu et de blanc
O Sainte Vierge
M'aimez-vous encore
Moi je sais bien
Que je vous aimerai
Jusqu'à ma mort
Et cependant c'est bien fini
Je ne crois plus au ciel ni à l'enfer
Je ne crois plus je ne crois plus
Le matelot qui fut sauvé
Pour n'avoir jamais oublié
De dire chaque jour un Ave
Me ressemblait me ressemblait

Prayer

When I was a little child
My mother always dressed me in blue and white
O Holy Virgin
Do you love me still
For my part I
Know I shall love you
Until I die
And yet it's finished all the same
I don't believe in heaven or in hell
I don't believe any more I don't believe
The sailor who was rescued
For never having forgotten to say
A Hail Mary every day
Looked like me he looked like me

Hôtel

Ma chambre a la forme d'une cage
Le soleil passe son bras par la fenêtre
Mais moi qui veux fumer pour faire des mirages
J'allume au feu du jour ma cigarette
Je ne veux pas travailler je veux fumer

Hotel

My room's shaped like a cage the sun
Puts his arm right through the window
But I who wish to smoke and dream
Use it to light my cigarette
I don't want to work I want to smoke

Calligramme à Madeleine (le 15 mai, 1915)

Le ciel est d'un bleu profond
Et mon regard s'y noie et fond

Un invisible obus miaule
J'écris assis au pied d'un saule

Calligram for Madeleine (15 May 1915)

The sky's as blue and black as ink
My eyes drown in it and sink

Darkness a shell whines over me
I write this under a willow tree

Le neuvième poème secret

J'adore ta toison qui est le parfait triangle
      De la Divinité
Je suis le bûcheron de l'unique forêt vierge
      O mon Eldorado
Je suis le seul poisson de ton océan voluptueux
      Toi ma belle sirène
Je suis l'alpiniste de tes montagnes neigeuses
      O mon alpe très blanche
Je suis l'archer divin de ta bouche si belle
      O mon très cher carquois
Et je suis le hâleur de tes cheveux nocturnes
      O beau navire sur le canal de mes baisers
Et les lys de tes bras m'appellent par des signes
      O mon jardin d'été
Les fruits de ta poitrine mûrissent pour moi leur douceur
      O mon verger parfumé
Et je te dresse ô Madeleine ô ma beauté sur le monde
      Comme la torche de toute lumière

The Ninth Secret Poem

I worship your fleece which is the perfect triangle
     Of the Goddess
I am the lumberjack of the only virgin forest
     O my Eldorado
I am the only fish in your voluptuous ocean
     You my lovely Siren
I am the climber on your snowy mountains
     O my whitest Alp
I am the heavenly archer of your beautiful mouth
     O my darling quiver
I am the hauler of your midnight hair
     O lovely ship on the canal of my kisses
And the lilies of your arms are beckoning me
     O my summer garden
The fruits of your breast are ripening their honey for me
     O my sweet-smelling orchard
And I am raising you O Madeleine O my beauty above the earth
     Like the torch of all light

Inscription pour le tombeau
du peintre Henri Rousseau Douanier

Gentil Rousseau tu nous entends
Nous te saluons
Delaunay sa femme Monsieur Queval et moi
Laisse passer nos bagages en franchise à la porte du ciel
Nous t'apporterons des pinceaux des couleurs des toiles
Afin que tes loisirs sacrés dans la lumière réelle
Tu les consacres à peindre comme tu tiras mon portrait
La face des étoiles

Inscription for the Tomb of the Painter
Henri Rousseau the Douanier

Kind Rousseau you who hear us now
We greet you
Delaunay his wife Monsieur Queval and I
Let our luggage pass freely through the customs-house of heaven
And we'll bring you brushes and colours and canvases
So that you may devote your holy leisure in the true light
To painting as you once did my portrait
The faces of the stars

Table

Ma table est rectangulaire, ses angles sont arrondis. Je fume la pipe bien que le tabac me dégoûte mais son amertume et sa brûlure me plaisent.

J'aurais voulu travailler ce matin mais je n'ai fait que fouiller de vieux brouillons à moi. Les machines où l'on adapte du papier buvard sont des trucs idiots, il vaut mieux sécher ce qu'on écrit avec du papier buvard non monté, c'est ce qu'il y a de mieux. Il est rose comme un visage fardé, peu à peu il noircit au centre rectangulairement. Maintenant je ne fais rien, j'écris ce que je vois, mon mouchoir est près de moi froissé. Il y a aussi une boite d'allumettes suédoises à l'envers, elle est vieux rose avec un cercle rouge où il y a un A un M et un C avec une torche allumée. Ça me fait penser aux réclames de chemin de fer qui furent le principal au paysage à mon dernier voyage en chemin de fer et quelles jolies rumeurs dans les poteaux électriques sur les routes où je me promenai tout le jour.

A

T T

E

N T

ION

DANGER DE MORT

C'était écrit sur ces poteaux plus émouvants qu'un mélo. Je m'embête. Je vais casser une pipe de terre qui est vraiment mauvaise, il faut aussi que je jette quelques pipes en bois qui jutent vraiment trop puis en pensant à plusieurs choses à la fois, ayant mal à la nuque, les yeux fixes je vais m'arracher des peaux autour des doigts et si je saigne je me sucerai le doigt jusqu'à ce que l'obscurité étant complète je me lèverai pour allumer une lampe.

Table

My table is oblong, its corners are round. I am smoking a pipe although the tobacco disgusts me: but its bitterness and burning please me.

I should have liked to work this morning but I have done nothing but rummage among my old drafts. Those things they fix blotting paper to are idiotic, it is better to dry what you have written with a piece of unmounted blotting paper: that is much the best. It is pink like a powdered face, little by little it goes black in the middle, rectangularly. Now I am doing nothing, I am writing what I see: my handkerchief is next to me, crumpled up. There is also a box of Swedish matches upside down, dull pink, with a red circle containing an A, an M, and a C, with a lighted torch. It reminds me of the posters next to the railway which were the main feature of the landscape on my last railway journey and what lovely sounds inside the electricity poles along the roads where I walked all day.

A

T T

E

N T

ION

DANGER DE MORT

That was what was written on those posts, more exciting than a melodrama. I am bored. I am going to break a clay pipe which is very bad, I shall also have to throw away some wooden pipes which have got altogether too juicy, then thinking about several things at the same time with a pain in my neck and my eyes staring at nothing I shall pull at the cuticles of my fingernails and if one bleeds I shall suck my finger until darkness being complete I get up to light a lamp.

'Voici le cerceuil ...'

```
VOICI
LE  CE
RCUEI
L  DAN
S  LEQ
UEL  I
L  GIS
AIT  P
OURR
ISSA
NT E
T    P
ALE
```

'Here is the coffin . . .'

```
       HERE
     IS THE C
     OFFIN IN
     WHICH H
      E  REST
      ED  RO
      TTING
      AND P
      A L L
```

'Vive la France!'

```
VIVE    LA    FRANCE!
IL   DORT  DANS   SON
PETIT  LIT   DE   SOL
DAT   MON  POETE   R
E          S        S
U                   S
C                   I
T                   E
```

'Endurcis-toi vieux cœur . . .'

Endurcis-toi vieux cœur entends les cris perçants
Que poussent les blessés au loin agonisants
Hommes poux de la terre ô vermine tenace

'Long live France!'

```
LONG    LIVE    FRANCE!
HE  SLEEPS  IN  HIS  LI
TTLE   SOLDIER'S   BED
MY         RESUSCITATED
P                      O
E                      T
```

'Harden old heart ...'

Harden old heart listen to the piercing cries
That the wounded in agony utter a long way off
O men lice of the earth tenacious vermin

[Poème épistolaire]

Premier canonnier conducteur
Je suis au front et te salue
Non non tu n'as pas la berlue
Cinquante-neuf est mon secteur

J'entends siffl_e_r
Le   l'oiseau
bel oiseau rapa^c^e

```
Je vois de loin        O        C
la cathédrale          M        H
                       O        E
                       N  A     R
                       N  D  R  E
                       B  I  L  L  Y
```

Letter to André Billy. 9 April 1915

Gunner / Driver One (front-line)
Here I am and send you greetings
No no you're not seeing things
My Sector's number fifty-nine

I hear the whistle of
the   the bird
beautiful bird of prey

I see far away
the cathedral

O   D
H   E
M   A
Y A R
N D R E
B I L L Y

Inscription qui se trouve
sur le tombeau d'Apollinaire

Je me suis enfin détaché
De toutes choses naturelles
Je peux mourir mais non pécher
Et ce qu'on n'a jamais touché
Je l'ai touché je l'ai palpé
Et j'ai scruté tout ce que nul
Ne peut en rien imaginer
Et j'ai soupesé maintes fois
Même la vie impondérable
Je peux mourir en souriant

Inscription
on Apollinaire's Tombstone

At last I have become detached
From every single natural thing
Now I can die but cannot sin
And what no one has ever touched
I have touched and felt it too
I have examined everything
That no one can at all imagine
I have weighed and weighed again
Even imponderable life
I can die and smile as well

Notes on the Poems

'Orpheus', 'Tortoise', 'Horse', 'Tibetan Goat', 'Hare', 'Rabbit', 'Dromedary', 'Mouse' and 'Carp' are taken from *Le Bestiaire*; 'Zone', 'The Pont Mirabeau', 'The Song of the Ill-Loved', 'Autumn Crocuses', 'Annie', 'Marizibill', 'The Traveller', 'The Door', 'The Circus People', 'The Landor Road Emigrant', 'Rosemonde', 'May', 'Synagogue', 'The Betrothal', '1909', 'In the Santé' and 'Hunting Horns' from *Alcools*; 'The Windows', 'Rue Christine Monday', 'Heart, Crown and Mirror', 'It's Raining', 'The Little Car', 'Gala', 'Exercise', 'Postcard' and 'The Pretty Red-Head' from *Calligrammes*; 'Cornflower' from *Il y a*; 'The Skirt', 'Prayer' and 'Hotel' from *Poèmes Divers* (1900–1917); 'Calligram for Madeleine (15 May 1915)' and 'The Ninth Secret Poem' from *Poèmes à Madeleine*; 'Inscription for the Tomb of the Painter Henri Rousseau the Douanier', 'Table', 'Here is the coffin …' and 'Harden old heart …' from *Poèmes Retrouvés*; 'Letter to André Billy' from *Poèmes Épistolaires*.

Apollinaire's poems are collected in a definitive edition published in 1956 by Gallimard, in the Pléiade series. They are divided, broadly speaking, into three books of poems (Le Bestiaire, Alcools, Calligrammes) *published during the poet's lifetime, and the posthumous collections* (Il y a, Le Guetteur Mélancolique, etc.). *This second group, together with the plays, bulks larger than the first; but it is by the books in the first group by and above all by* Alcools – *that Apollinaire is most widely known.*

The poems from Le Bestiaire, *Apollinaire's earliest collection, are dispersed throughout the book for decorative purposes. All other material is arranged in strict conformity with the Pléiade order.*

Le Bestiaire, ou Cortège d'Orphée (*The Bestiary, or Procession of Orpheus*) *was begun in 1906 and published in 1911. An* édition de luxe *in the best sense of the phrase, it was hand-printed and illustrated with wood engravings by Raoul Dufy.* (*Picasso was to have supplied the pictures, but only got as far as doing the first two engravings of animals: an eagle and a chicken. These were not used.*) *The first edition consisted of only 120 copies, most of which remained unsold.* Le Bestiaire *is a modern version of the medieval bestiaries: a book of marvels containing not only domestic and exotic, but mythological animals, linked together by images of Orpheus. Altogether there are thirty pictures, each with its accompanying short poem. These are followed by Apollinaire's own notes.*

ORPHEUS (p. 19)

Interspersed throughout the sequence of animal poems in the *Bestiaire* are a series of 'Orpheus' poems. This one is the first in the book. Trismegistus is of course Hermes Trismegistus, 'the Egyptian priest and philosopher, and the supposed author of 40 books on theology, medicine, and geography' (Lemprière). The poem celebrates the woodcuts of the original edition, by Dufy.

TORTOISE (p. 34)

'Orpheus . . . a native of Thrace . . . played a lyre which Mercury had given him. It was formed of the shell of a tortoise . . .' (from Apollinaire's own notes to the *Bestiaire*).

HORSE (p. 35)

The illustration is of Pegasus.

Alcools *(spirits – in the sense of 'hard liquor')* * *appeared in 1913, with a portrait of the author by Picasso. It consists, roughly, of four sorts of poems: poems dating from his stay on the Rhine, where he met Annie Playden, who was employed as a governess in the same household in which Apollinaire was tutor; poems written subsequently, inspired by his love for Annie Playden; poems celebrating – or inspired by the vicissitudes of – his love for Marie Laurencin; and, finally, his whole output of various poems written between 1898 and 1908. Standing rather apart from these, there is the poem called 'Zone', which was introduced into the proofs of Alcools at the last moment, at the same time at which Apollinaire removed every single punctuation mark from the book. The word Zone is applied to the military zone surrounding Paris: a non-built-up area maintained for the purpose of defence. The poem stands first in the text of Alcools, and serves to mark off the present (I mean of course the 'present' in 1913) from the past, in terms both of Apollinaire's personal life:*

You suffered love at twenty years old and at thirty

– and of his attitude to life:

In the end you are tired of that world of antiquity
O Eiffel Tower shepherdess the bridges this morning are
a bleating flock

---

* See lines 7 and 8 from the end of 'Zone' for a possible elucidation of this title.

Alcools stands at the centre of Apollinaire's poetry – flanked as it were on the one hand by the charming Bestiaire, *and on the other by the more provocative* Calligrammes.

ZONE (p. 21)

The habit of addressing himself as 'you' is very noticeable in Apollinaire. It occurs constantly in this poem; and quite surprisingly (line 27) on the second occasion, since he is in the middle of talking about the 'pretty street whose name I forget'.

The girl whose image 'persists through anguish and insomnia' (lines 86–8) is presumed to be Marie Laurencin.

In line 92, Apollinaire makes a joke of the endings of words formed from the names of towns (Nice, Menton, La Turbie), and mixes them up, as if we should say: A Mancudlian, a Liverpooler, an Edinburgher.

Line 99: The agates of St Vitus's cathedral are a mixture of precious and semi-precious stones on the walls of the St Wenceslas Chapel, in one of which (an amethyst) Apollinaire says he saw his own face 'with flaming demented eyes'. '"It's my face," I shouted, "with my dark jealous eyes!" We had to leave. I was pale and unhappy from seeing myself thus mad – I who have always been afraid of losing my reason.' (Quoted from 'Le Passant de Prague', the first story in *L'Hérésiarque et Cie*.)

The Examining Magistrate's (line 113) is presumably the office in which Apollinaire was interrogated when he was accused of being a party to the theft of certain sculptures from the Louvre. He did in fact spend a week in solitary confinement in the Santé prison on suspicion of being implicated in this affair.

THE SONG OF THE ILL-LOVED (p. 37)

Line 63: 'her I lost before / in Germany' is certainly Annie Playden, whom Apollinaire first met and courted there.

Line 158: 'O daughters of the Argive king' – the Danaïds, whose eternal punishment in hell was to fill with water a vessel full of holes.

AUTUMN CROCUSES (p. 63)

Meadow-saffron is a more correct translation of the title in the original, 'Les colchiques'. These flowers are named after the island of Colchis, the birthplace of Medea; and a place, as Lemprière says, 'fruitful in poisonous herbs'. Hence *colchicum*.

ANNIE (p. 65)

This is presumably a fantasy about Annie Playden, who left England to go to America (partly to escape Apollinaire's pursuit of her) in 1904. This poem first appeared in 1912.

THE TRAVELLER (p. 69)

'*Euripus*, a narrow strait which separates the island of Euboea from the coast of Boeotia. Its flux and reflux, which continued regular during eighteen or nineteen days, and were commonly unsettled the rest of the month, were a matter of deep inquiry among the ancients; and it is said that Aristotle threw himself into it because he was unable to find out the causes of that phenomenon' – *Lemprière's Classical Dictionary*.

THE DOOR (p. 73)

Pi-mus are the fish which are the counterparts of the birds called *pi-his* (see the part of 'Zone' which talks about the birds and the aeroplanes: lines 53–70).

THE LANDOR ROAD EMIGRANT (p. 79)

Line 28: A popular saying in a storm is: 'The devil is beating his wife and marrying off his daughter.' Apollinaire has presumably based his line on this saying.

MAY (p. 85)

This poem and the one following, 'Synagogue', are taken from a group of poems entitled *Rhénanes*, which are among the poems dating from Apollinaire's stay on the Rhine.

SYNAGOGUE (p. 87)

A friend in Jerusalem, Gideon Cohen, comments that Ottomar and Abraham may have felt some pride in fulfilling their Sabbath obligation, and some superiority, but *no anger* and *no envy* of what a Christian is permitted to do on the Sabbath. He doubts that they would be quarrelling, since there are strict rules about behaviour on the way to prayer. He concludes that this strange poem is an essay in exoticism, including the combination of Hebrew quotations at the close: 'He who wreaks vengeance on the Gentiles and punishment on peoples.'

Loulavim: the bunches of palm, myrtle, willow and citrus which are taken into the synagogue on Succot.

THE BETROTHAL (p. 89)

This poem was written during the unhappiest period of Apollinaire's life, after his arrest and release from the Santé prison (see conclusion of note on 'Zone', above), and his final break with Marie Laurencin. The dedication may or may not have some bearing on the part Picasso played in the 'affair of the statues'. The poem as a whole appears to be an attempt to purge melancholy with fire. Fire images abound in it, but its atmosphere generally is of the blackest despair.

IN THE SANTÉ (p. 101)

See conclusion of note on 'Zone', above.

Calligrammes *was published in* 1918. *The poems in it were written between* 1912 *and* 1917. *It is in six sections. The first, consisting of poems of* peacetime, was to have appeared under the title Et moi aussi je suis peintre ('And I, too, am a painter'). *The remaining five sections were written in wartime. They have titles like* Étendards *('Banners') and* Lueurs des Tirs *('Flashes of Gunfire'). Most of the poems in* Calligrammes *are not 'calligrams' but poems in conventional typographical forms; but the inclusion in this book of poems which were also pictures made it seem a very unusual book indeed. Apollinaire's explanation is an interesting one, though it does not really 'justify' the experiments. (See page* 6 *– not that any justification is necessary.)*

THE WINDOWS (p. 111)

Composed in 1913, for a catalogue of paintings by Robert Delaunay (see also page 153), this was one of Apollinaire's favourite poems. It began as an improvisation between Apollinaire and two friends in a café, where Apollinaire suddenly remembered that he was late with his copy for the catalogue (see line 5), and it was finished in Delaunay's studio (where the yellow shoes were: line 18). In the last three lines I imagine Delaunay's window slowly opening on a wintry landscape in Paris, until it catches the big orange sun: everything goes from cold to hot, from North to South, from shadow to dazzling light. But possibly I read too much into it.

For *pi-his*, see note on 'The Door'.

RUE CHRISTINE MONDAY (p. 115)

Presumably almost all of this poem is verbatim speech from various conversations in a café. The last line of the poem is highly ambiguous: its literal meaning is the only one I give; but in addition it is a slang expression for a blow in the face; and it is also an oblique reference to syphilis.

HEART, CROWN AND MIRROR (p. 119)

See note on 'Inscription on Apollinaire's Tombstone' below.

THE LITTLE CAR (p. 123)

The first line is an echo of a popular song. (The date is incorrect, presumably for this reason.)

Pouhon: Walloon word meaning chalybeate or iron-impregnated spring such as occurs in the Spa district of Belgium. There is one of these between the stream called Eau Rouge and the Stavelot road, near Francorchamps. (For the foregoing explanation, given on the authority of Maurice Piron ['Les Wallonismes de Guillaume Apollinaire', from *Mélanges de linguistique Française offerts à M. Charles Bruneau*, 1954], I am indebted to M. Michel Décaudin.)

THE PRETTY RED-HEAD (p. 135)

'Be lenient when you compare us'. This and the two lines which follow are inscribed on six steles surrounding the Apollinaire monument between Stavelot and Spa.

CORNFLOWER (p. 139)

Paper cornflowers, 'Bleuets de France', are sold in France on 11 November and correspond to our Remembrance Day poppies.

PRAYER (p. 145)

Line 2: See also line 26 of 'Zone' (line 2 of page 23).

THE NINTH SECRET POEM (p. 151)

One of a series of more or less erotic poems to Madeleine Pagès, whom Apollinaire met in January 1915 in a train going from Nice to Marseille. This poem occurs in a letter to Madeleine dated 12 November 1915, from the front.

INSCRIPTION FOR THE TOMB OF THE PAINTER
HENRI ROUSSEAU THE DOUANIER (p. 153)

Monsieur Queval was Rousseau's landlord; Robert Delaunay is mentioned in the note about 'The Windows' (see above). Rousseau did indeed paint Apollinaire's portrait: he stands next to Marie Laurencin under some 'tropical' trees (or perhaps they are a kind of ash tree) with a white quill pen in one hand and a scroll in the other. There is a row of sweet william (*œillets du poète*) at their feet.

INSCRIPTION ON APOLLINAIRE'S TOMBSTONE (p. 163)

In the Père Lachaise Cemetery, and together with the Heart (from 'Heart, Crown and Mirror'), these lines are cut into Apollinaire's tombstone. They are in fact two five-line stanzas run together, from a long poem called 'Les collines', in *Calligrammes*

It would be difficult, even if it were appropriate, to give in these short notes a complete catalogue of Apollinaire's works. Apart from the poems, there are books of stories and fantasy of extraordinary interest, like L'Hérésiarque et Cie *and* Le Poète Assassiné; *a collection of articles and anecdotes about Paris:* Le Flâneur des Deux Rives; *and two well-known erotic novels which were published in translation by the Olympia Press under the title* The Debauched Hospodar *and* Memoirs of a Young Rakehell. *There are, besides all this, the play* Les Mamelles de Tirésias *(Tiresias' Breasts), first produced in 1917, and produced in 1947 set to music by Poulenc; Apollinaire's edition of the first anthology of the works of De Sade, published in 1909, and of various other eighteenth-century writers; and, finally, the* Futurist Manifesto *of 1913. All this adds to the confusion; but it also adds force to André Billy's use of the word Baroque (see page 7) to describe Apollinaire.*

Verse &c.

Verse &c. collects a substantial body of Oliver Bernard's poetry written since the early 1980s and the publication of *Poems* (1983). The volume offers lyricism, narratives, political protest, poems about people, poems of place, an anonymous Middle English poem, and much else. Bernard's wit and clarity of imagination will surprise and delight.

'At the heart of it is a wonderful version of the anonymous Middle English poem *Quia Amore Langueo*. The best of Bernard can be said to aspire to a comparable anonymity. His poems have real originality, and convey a strong sense of the particulars of his own existence, yet at the same time they rise to moments when they ring with a music that seems almost remembered. . . . one of the most natural and accomplished of living poets'
— Robert Nye, *The Tablet*

'[His] poems have a strong, musical humanity, something plumbed and opened, which I find very admirable'
— Brendan Kennelly

Rimbaud: The Poems

Oliver Bernard's *Rimbaud* was first published in 1962. This newly revised edition of his superb presentation adds the Latin verse which Rimbaud wrote as school exercises. The poems are presented in bilingual form with Bernard's lively and accurate prose versions below the French. Together with an illuminating introduction and the inclusion of a selection of Rimbaud's letters, this is the most useful presentation of Rimbaud's astonishing body of work for English-language readers.

French Poetry from Anvil

Charles Baudelaire
Translated and introduced by Francis Scarfe
Volume I: The Complete Verse
Volume II: Paris Blues (The Poems in Prose) *with 'La Fanfarlo'*

Francis Scarfe's prose versions of the complete poetry of France's greatest nineteenth-century poet are both scrupulous and inventive. 'No one must underestimate the value of the present enterprise to even the most advanced student of French literature.'
– Michael Glover, *British Book News*

Tristan Corbière: Wry-Blue Loves
Translated and introduced by Peter Dale

'... there are not many men who have written poems as good as his, and he can wait in mocking confidence for the world to make its way to his grave.' – RANDALL JARRELL

As Peter Dale writes in his introduction: 'Above all, he is his own man, able to resist the blandishments of literary theory, social expectations, and the mollifications of religion.'

Jean Follain: 130 Poems
Translated and introduced by Christopher Middleton

The poetry of Jean Follain (1903–1971) is increasingly seen, by poets and critics in France and by his foreign admirers, as central to French poetry's change of course after Surrealism. Christopher Middleton, the distinguished poet and translator, has chosen poems spanning Follain's entire writing life, and has written an illuminating introduction to his elegant translations.

Victor Hugo: The Distance, The Shadows
Translated and introduced by Harry Guest

In this new edition of his acclaimed translations, Harry Guest convincingly brings into English many of Hugo's great qualities: his passion for social justice, his simple humanity and an imaginative breadth of vision which few poets have equalled.

Poems of Jules Laforgue
Translated and introduced by Peter Dale

Peter Dale captures Laforgue's wit and panache in this substantial selection from one of the quirkiest and most entertaining of French poets. 'Generally, when Dale adapts, he still manages to reproduce, conveying much of the letter of the original as well as the spirit. . . . The collection is hard to over-praise' – D. J. Enright, *The Observer*

Gérard de Nerval: The Chimeras
Translated by Peter Jay
with an essay by Richard Holmes

'The rendering of Gérard de Nerval's justly celebrated and mysteriously allusive sonnet sequence in English is a formidably difficult enterprise, and translator and publisher are to be congratulated.' – Michael Glover, *Books and Bookmen*

Jacques Réda: The Mirabelle Pickers
Translated by Jennie Feldman

In this delightful prose memoir, Jacques Réda chooses the height of the plum-picking season to revisit his home town in Lorraine, north-eastern France. The fragrant allure of mirabelles introduces vividly remembered places that have shaped a lifetime's writing, and a colourful mix of old acquaintances renewed in these five days.

Jacques Réda: Treading Lightly
Translated by Jennie Feldman

The first English selection of Jacques Réda's poems draws on his earliest major collections, widely regarded as among his finest: *Amen*, awarded the Prix Max Jacob, 1968; *Récitatif*, 1970; and *La Tourne*, 1975. 'He is indisputably one of the most invigorating French writers' – John Taylor, *Paths to Contemporary French Literature*

Arthur Rimbaud: A Season in Hell and Other Poems
Translated by Norman Cameron
with an introduction by Michael Hamburger

In the opinion of Robert Graves, Norman Cameron was unsurpassed as a translator of Rimbaud. This volume contains thirty-three of the verse poems and the whole of *Une Saison en enfer*, the extraordinary work that was Rimbaud's literary testament, his apology, and a contribution to the mythology of his time.

Paul Verlaine: Women/Men
Femmes/Hombres
Translated by Alistair Elliot

'... in Verlaine's clandestine collections of erotic verse, Mr Elliot succeeds marvellously ... astonishing, beautiful poems, astonishingly and beautifully rendered.' – D. M. Thomas

Paul Valéry: Charms *and Other Pieces*
Translated and introduced by Peter Dale

Paul Valéry's most celebrated collection *Charmes* was published in 1922 and quickly achieved classic status. Peter Dale's versions offer a fresh view of an intriguing poet, now somewhat neglected but here revived in English.

Poems of François Villon
Translated and introduced by Peter Dale

Peter Dale's remarkable translation is now reissued in much revised form. Holding close to Villon's rhyme-schemes and metres, he gives us the vigour, wit, charm and pathos of this thrilling medieval poet.

Into the Deep Street
SEVEN MODERN FRENCH POETS
Translated and introduced by Jennie Feldman and Stephen Romer

Includes Jean Follain, Henri Thomas, Philippe Jaccottet, Jacques Réda, Paul de Roux, Guy Goffette, Gilles Ortlieb. From the key figure of Jean Follain, who can freeze an entire period of history in a vignette of a few lines, via the best-known of the close-knit if regionally scattered group, Philippe Jaccottet, to the newer voices of Guy Goffette and Gilles Ortlieb, all these poets are masters of wry brevity and the resonant image.

These books are bilingual except Jean Follain: *130 Poems* and Jacques Réda: *The Mirabelle Pickers*.

www.anvilpresspoetry.com